Teaching
Like Jesus

A Practical Guide to

Christian Education

in Your Church

La Verne Tolbert

ZondervanPublishingHouse
Grand Rapids, Michigan

A Division of HarperCollinsPublishers

Teaching Like Jesus
Copyright © 2000 by La Verne Tolbert

Requests for information should be addressed to:

■ Zondervan Publishing House
Grand Rapids, Michigan 49530

Library of Congress Cataloging-in-Publication Data

Tolbert, La Verne.
    Teaching like Jesus : a practical guide to Christian education in your church /
La Verne Tolbert.
        cm.
    ISBN 0-310-22347-4 (pbk.)
    1. Christian education—Teaching methods. 2. Jesus Christ—Teaching
methods. I. Title.
BV1534.T59   1999
268—dc21   99-39364
                                                                              CIP

On page 90, "Is God Calling You?" by Don Stabler is used by permission of the author.

On page 169, "As the Deer" by Martin Nystrom © 1984 Maranatha Praise, Inc. (Administered by the Copyright Company, Nashville, TN). All rights reserved. International copyright secured. Used by permission.

On page 184, "So I Send You" by E. Margaret Clarkson © 1954 Singspiration Music/ASCAP. All rights reserved. Reprinted by special permission of Brentwood-Benson Music Publishing, Inc.

All Scripture quotations, except in appendix B and unless otherwise noted, are taken from the HOLY BIBLE: NEW INTERNATIONAL VERSION®. Copyright © 1973, 1978, 1984 by International Bible Society. Used by permission of Zondervan Publishing House. All rights reserved.

Interior design by Jody DeNeef and Nancy Wilson

Printed in the United States of America

99 00 01 02 03 04 05 /❖ DC/ 10 9 8 7 6 5 4 3 2 1

To My Family

To Irving, my husband, for loving me so

To La Nej, my daughter, my joy and star student

To Aunt Valerie Henderson for teaching me the value
of resting and rejoicing

To Aunt Lorraine and Uncle David for passing the
faith baton to the next generation

To my mother-in-the-Lord, Anna Wallick, for daily
calling my name before the Father

To the Family of Faith where he has planted me to run this race

And to my parents and grandparents, peering over
heaven's balcony, cheering me on

Contents

List of Illustrations

Acknowledgments

Teachers come and go. But many stay. I humbly thank all of the teachers with whom I have worked, and especially those volunteers who have clocked more than 10 years in the classroom on Sunday mornings. They include Diane Alexander, Saundra Coleman, LeTaun Cole Cotton, Delores Gilford, Joyce Hudgies, Marvin Jackson, La Roya Jordan, Clotee McAfee, Donald Sanderson, Mamie Shelton, Janice Webb, Alice Williams, and Debra Willis. You represent the thousands of men and women in local churches across this country who energetically and with excellence are committed to making disciples. Thank you for your faithfulness.

For their invaluable comments on the manuscript, I extend a sincere thank you to my dear friend and mentor, Dr. Shelly Cunningham, Assistant Professor of Christian Education at Talbot School of Theology; Dr. Pete Menjares, Chair of the Education Department at Biola University; my colleague and friend, Linda Paek (such detail!); Gala Christian, Demetra Pearson, Janice Webb, and Beverly Winton.

Stan Gundry, editor-in-chief, who patiently coaxed this work out of me, receives my deepest gratitude. My editor, Jim Ruark, whose enthusiasm and seasoned insight propelled me, has earned my heartfelt appreciation. Finally, to all of those who have taught me—from Sunday school to seminary—thank you for depositing within me an incomparable love for teaching God's Word.

Chapter 1

What Is Christian Education?
A Philosophy of Ministry

> And the things which you have heard from me in the presence of many witnesses, these entrust to faithful men, who will be able to teach others also.
>
> 2 Timothy 2:2 NASB

Teaching is our ministry. Jesus is our model. People are our passion. Transformed lives are our product. And heaven is our goal. This is the essence of Christian education.

My journey into the ministry of teaching in the local church is actually rooted in my childhood. My hero—my dad—was our pastor. As the dutiful daughter, I assumed the task of teaching Sunday school to our handful of children, training the teachers, and giving leadership to our youth ministry.

Ours was a very small church, a storefront to be exact, just two blocks from 125th Street in New York City. Dad was an evangelist at heart, and he was creative about building a congregation. He had rigged a loudspeaker to the street outside and connected it to the pulpit microphone so that passersby could hear the preaching.

An additional benefit of our loudspeaker system was that people on the sidewalks could also hear the choir, which my mother directed. Admittedly, ours was a small choir, but under her tutelage we sounded as voluminous as any mass choir, and in choir competitions we either won or came in second.

Grandmother knew how to pray. "It's me again, Lord," was the personal familiarity with which she addressed her God. And she could sing. Her operatic voice had been featured on the Refuge Temple radio program, and although she no longer performed, her praises bellowed from the pews.

Mother Inniss, as she was lovingly known, was ever the faithful mother-in-law. She had left the glamour of her thousand-member church home to help her son-in-law pioneer his ministry. She passed her musical talent on to her daughters, Leanore, Lorraine, and Esther, who were known as the Inniss Sisters. And my mother, Leanore, conveyed all that she had learned to the choir. So the combination of a preaching-teaching ministry coupled with good ol' gospel music promised to be an excellent foundation for the building of a church.

But it was hard work, and despite the influx of new members, the congregation never grew beyond a few handfuls of dedicated people. If success is measured in numbers, then the impact of our little church is questionable. But if success is measured by changed lives, what a crown Daddy received when he saw Jesus face-to-face!

Because we were small, losing a member was major. Perhaps the biggest exodus came when one of the single women in our church had become pregnant. The newly converted wallowed in righteous indignation. They demanded that my father throw this young woman out of the church. His calm response came in the form of a question: "Why would I throw her out now when she needs us the most?" Dad's sensitive, compassionate ability to embrace those who were suffering emanated from his own life so overshadowed with pain and disappointment. Like Jesus, my father chose understanding rather than condemnation.

My dad's passion was to see his members "set free." Sister Gadson, for example, had a phobia of riding in cars and busses. She was terrified at the thought. Consequently, she never traveled beyond walking distance of her apartment in the projects. But Dad was convinced of the reality of Scripture, "If the Son sets you free, you will be free indeed" (John 8:36).

"Get in the car," he demanded one day. "No, pastor," Sister Gadson meekly refused. But because of her respect for him, she eventually obliged. Dad drove her and her husband around Manhattan, and she loved it! The fear of traveling was gone.

Entering the Ministry

Personally, I had no intentions of entering the ministry. In fact, I had promised myself that I would never marry a pastor. I had no illusions about the work involved. Up close, the demands of pastoring seemed overwhelming.

On call day and night, Dad was often summoned from sleep to an emergency at the hospital, or to a home to calm disputes, or to the jail to help a member's child who was in trouble. There never seemed time for him to really rest. On many nights after a full day of hard physical labor as a carpenter, Dad would shower, change clothes, and drive from New Rochelle to Manhattan to teach Bible classes or to play the piano or organ during choir rehearsal or to conduct meetings.

A Bible school graduate, Dad's preaching and teaching style was exegetical. He taught what the Scriptures said and then applied them to today. Always, Dad ministered with his whole heart. I came to love the Lord dearly and trust him completely because of the absolute faith that my father placed in his Savior.

I taught Sunday school. Soon I became frustrated with the curriculum available. Here we were teaching in a one-room church with several classes occurring simultaneously. These children lived in the inner city in tall buildings and walked through snow to school. But the pictures on the covers of most Sunday school material featured lovely country homes with picket fences and rosy children with smiling faces. They resembled no one in our congregation. Out of frustration, I began writing and developing our own lessons. Little did I realize that I was in God's preparatory school.

After a 10-year stint on Madison Avenue as a magazine editor, God's call on my life began to materialize. Although I had reached the top and had experienced tremendous success, I felt empty inside. All of the hard work and all of the extra hours struggling to "make it" did not produce the fulfillment it had promised.

One Sunday, my brother, Elder Allen Powlis, preached a sermon from Mark 11:22, "Have faith in God." It haunted me. Of course I had faith in God! I was raised in a Christian home, accepted Christ as my Savior, was baptized according to Scripture, taught Sunday school, sang in the choir, worked with the youth, and served on the Pastor's Aide Committee.

At home, I read the passage again—"Have faith in God." "I do, I do have faith in God," I silently protested. The Holy Spirit whispered in my heart, "Have faith in God's *ability*." Through sheer willpower, I had become a self-made woman. My faith rested in my own reasoning, and I was dependent on fulfilling my own personal ambition.

Challenged to completely dedicate my life to God, I relocated to Los Angeles where I attended seminary. Now, so thirsty for God and straining to really know him for myself, I could hardly study the Bible enough, and I fell more in love with the teaching ministry.

The Boomerang

In one small-group teaching session, I experienced what I call a "biblical boomerang." It was my turn to lead the Bible study. The passage that God put on my heart concerned Jesus' discussion with Peter.

> When they had finished eating, Jesus said to Simon Peter, "Simon son of John, do you truly love me more than these?"
>
> "Yes, Lord," he said, "you know that I love you."
>
> Jesus said, "Feed my lambs."
>
> Again Jesus said, "Simon son of John, do you truly love me?"
>
> He answered, "Yes, Lord, you know that I love you."
>
> Jesus said, "Take care of my sheep."
>
> The third time he said to him, "Simon son of John, do you love me?"
>
> Peter was hurt because Jesus asked him the third time, "Do you love me?" He said, "Lord, you know all things; you know that I love you."
>
> Jesus said, "Feed my sheep."
>
> —JOHN 21:15–17

As I studied, I was struck with the phrase, "more than these," in verse 15. Did Peter love Jesus more than *what*?

Earlier in the day, Peter and his former business partners (Luke 5:10) had a board meeting (John 21:3). They had survived the traumatic events of the past few weeks, and now Jesus, crucified and risen, was no longer with them daily. They had only seen him twice since his resurrection, but they were about to see him for a third time (v. 14).

Before this next encounter, however, Peter had a decision to make. What on earth was he to do with his life now? Peter convinced his partners to return to their former profession. It's as if he concluded that the past three years had been a wonderful experience, but now it was time to get on with his life and go back to work. His partners agreed, and out they sailed. That night, however, the business failed; the fishermen caught nothing.

The next morning, Peter saw someone standing on the shore, but he did not realize that it was Jesus. This man asked Peter if they had caught any fish. Peter called back, "No." He was instructed to toss the net to the other side of the boat. Because a person standing on the shore could often see the schools of fish better than the fishermen in the boat, Peter obliged. With the unexpected, enormous catch, John shouted his realization—"It is the Lord!" Peter dove off the boat and swam to the shore where Jesus had a fire waiting.

Can you imagine that heavenly breakfast of fried fish and bread? After an unproductive night, Peter and his associates enjoyed a wonderful meal beside their huge catch—153 large fish, to be exact (v. 11). It was probably Peter who counted them! He may have concluded that if their catches continued like this one, their fishing business would be phenomenal.

More Than These

After breakfast, however, Jesus offered Peter a different proposition. He began by asking Peter if he loved him more than "these." The question now is, To what or to whom does "these" refer? Certainly, Jesus couldn't be comparing Peter's love for him to that of the other disciples. John, who also shared that morning's feast, had demonstrated his great love for Christ by remaining close by his side on the night that Jesus was arrested. It was John who stood at the foot of the cross with Mary (John 19:26). So Jesus could not be asking Peter if he loved him more than the other disciples loved him, because John sat among them.

Then to what did Jesus compare Peter's love? Knowing that Peter had decided to return to his profession as a fisherman, imagine Jesus pointing to the small mountain of fish and asking, "Peter, do you love me more than you love your fishing business? Do you love me more than you love these fish?"

Peter's ultimate response transformed him from a fisherman to a fisher of men as Jesus had promised when he initially recruited Peter and his brother Andrew (Matt. 4:19). Peter's vocation had now become his avocation. Pastor Peter's new career was to serve Christ by feeding his lambs and sheep.

As I taught this lesson, I could hear the Lord asking me to also make a choice. Would I leave my vocation to feed his lambs and sheep? The "Yes" did not come easily. I thought I had my life all figured out, and now, well into my thirties, I was facing a major career change.

Romans 12:1–2 had become the cornerstone verse of my commitment to Christ. Prayerfully, and through the benefit of wise counsel, I accepted the call. I decided to trust God with the results.

At the church I had been visiting, Pastor Kenneth Ulmer would interrupt the service every Sunday morning to plead with the congregation. He would say, "We need five more volunteers to help with the children. Now we need four more ... three ..." And so he would continue until there were enough workers for the nursery and children's church.

I thought to myself, "What a tragedy!" These adult saints need to catch the vision, for one of the most blessed opportunities we have is ministering to children! God had placed such a burden on my heart that during my prayer times, I found myself interceding for this ministry.

One morning, after confirmation with my prayer partner, I wrote a letter to the pastor asking how I could volunteer my services to help implement some new ideas. With the hand-delivered letter I included a large stack of educational materials that I had developed over the years. That Sunday, four days after I had placed my stack of material on the desk of pastor's secretary, I reluctantly joined the church during the early morning service.

The altar call was the longest I had ever heard, or so it felt. Although I wanted to help, I had not considered actually becoming a member of this congregation. The church was crowded, parking was poor, and the benches were hard. Visiting my friends here was fine, but joining? Just exactly what did God have in mind?

The pastor's final plea pricked my heart. "If you have a desire to work in this ministry, you need to be a member," he said to no one in particular. I marched down the aisle still wrestling with where God was leading me, wanting so much to have him spell out his complete plan for me in detail.

That Tuesday I received a call from the pastor's secretary. She made an appointment for me to meet with him at the church office the next day. He had read through all of my material, and in the meeting, much to my surprise, he offered me the job of Pastor of Christian Education.

"We thought it would be a man," he candidly admitted, "but you are obviously God's choice." Although I was surprised by the offer, I was more in awe of God. He really was serious about calling *me* into full-time ministry!

A few summers later, I was also asked to teach in the Christian Education Department at Talbot School of Theology. My dear friend and mentor, Dr. Shelly Cunningham, who has the reputation as one of the most creative teachers on campus, recommended me as an assistant professor. While still a student, I had volunteered as her teacher's assistant in the classroom, and a warm bond of mutual respect formed between us.

My cup overflowed! In addition to working in the local church, God entrusted me with the task of training teachers—men and women who came to the United States from countries all over the world to become better equipped as Sunday school teachers, Bible study leaders, small-group leaders, missionaries, and education pastors! What an honor! And what an awesome responsibility!

It is this combination of shared experience, a seasoned blend of principle and practice, that I humbly pass on to you. My prayer is that your school, church, ministry, pastors, teachers, parents, and volunteers will continue to become all that God intends. He has a plan! And it's perfect!

God does have a sense of humor. Instead of marrying a pastor, I became one. I reached up to heaven and caught Dad's mantle.

In cooperation with the Holy Spirit, Christian education is perhaps one of the most important ministries in the local church today. As Christian educators, we teach classes, train teachers, develop new ministries, design curriculum, and in general, oversee every area under our leadership. We are called to make "disciples."

> Therefore go and make disciples of all nations, baptizing them in the name of the Father and of the Son and of the Holy Spirit, and teaching them to obey everything I have commanded you. And surely I am with you always, to the very end of the age.
>
> —MATTHEW 28:19–20

To make disciples is to make "learners." We are to make men, women, and children into disciples of Jesus—learners after God's own heart—by teaching them to love, respect, and obey God and to live their lives in accordance with biblical principles. Because teachers have authority from God, they are important instruments through which the Holy Spirit matures the body of Christ. By assisting students to study, to think, to reason, and to perceive the reality of God by understanding the person of Christ, teachers fulfill the Great Commission.

Whom Do We Teach?

Jesus asked Peter to feed his lambs (John 21:15), and then he asked Peter to feed his sheep (21:16–17). The scope of the teaching ministry of the local church ranges from feeding lambs to feeding sheep. Our ministry is to teach children, who are the lambs, and to teach teenagers and adults, the sheep.

We teach children because we believe they are able to know Christ. Though they are the littlest people, they are big in God's eyes. It was a child by whom Jesus stood when asked who was the greatest among the disciples.

> Whoever welcomes this little child in my name welcomes me; and whoever welcomes me welcomes the one who sent me. For he who is least among you all—he is the greatest.
>
> —LUKE 9:48

Again Jesus stressed the importance of children when the disciples tried to clear his daily planner.

> Jesus said, "Let the little children come to me, and do not hinder them, for the kingdom of heaven belongs to such as these."
>
> —MATTHEW 19:14

We must allow children access to Christ. This means that we need to teach children in ways they can understand.

No matter how young, children are rational beings created in the image of God. They should be encouraged to study the Bible, and because they are children, they should have fun in the process of studying! Their learning experience should be exciting and enjoyable.

With the challenges consuming preteens and teenagers in the inner city, the demands for dynamic Christian education are greater than ever. Our youth should be salt and light (Matt. 5:13–14), which are metaphors of vitality and vision. Our teaching must empower them to do more than just survive. They must flourish in a world that is hostile to God and plagued with social injustices.

Unfortunately for many teens, these are the years when the teaching they receive is sometimes farthest from their reality. With the roadblocks of drugs, sex, and gangs, or with the obstacles of cultural assimilation, teens may tend to disengage from Christianity, feeling it irrelevant. The lifesaving truth of God's Word may become blurred in the face of the problems and temptations they face daily.

In many instances, when we teach, we are answering questions teens are not asking. The challenge is this: If we lose them now, it may take years for them to find their way back to the church steps. Our charge is one we must take seriously. It means that we must constantly evaluate how we teach to keep in step with their "now."

Adults, too, are caught in a social maze. Finding answers to their questions about their families, finances, and future can be framed within the context of a Christian worldview. Although not simplistic, teaching adults seems easy. They are able to sit longer, pay closer attention, and understand our teaching material.

However, the charge to feed adults is one that needs reexamination in the wake of ethical inconsistencies. Abortion is legal; homosexuality is tolerated; and sexual experimentation is the norm. In the midst of this world parents are expected to conduct their lives righteously and raise Christian children. We must bring honest dialogue and relevant teaching into our classrooms, "scratching" men and women where they itch. In other words, we must meet them at their point of need.

In addition, Christian education includes teaching the teacher. We train Sunday school teachers, Bible study teachers, youth leaders, new members teachers, discipleship counselors, small-group leaders—everyone who comes in contact with the learner. Our task is to impart skills that enhance the teaching gift. Our task is to challenge these Christian leaders to lifestyles of holiness. And our task is to encourage excellence and demand that teachers and leaders become students of the Word. Where appropriate, we encourage some would-be teachers to attend Bible college or seminary.

These are the "who" in the Christian educator's classroom. As Christian educators we disciple disciples.

What Do We Teach?

In Christian education, we teach God's Word. The Bible is our curriculum, our primary textbook. Any other curriculum is secondary.

We teach the Bible because we believe that it is understandable. In fact, it is our responsibility, our task to teach the Bible so that it is *understood*. Jesus stressed the importance of the learner's understanding in the parable of the soils (Matt. 13). The evil one snatches away the Word from the hearts of those who do not understand the message.

> But the one who received the seed that fell on good soil is the man who hears the word and understands it. He produces a crop, yielding a hundred, sixty or thirty times what was sown.
>
> —Matthew 13:23

It is not enough that learners "hear" our teaching. They must understand what they hear. God's principles can, and should, have practical application to their lives. Once they understand, the seed of the Word will bear fruit.

When and Where Do We Teach?

Christian education supplements the morning worship teaching-preaching hours with purposeful, ongoing classes on Sunday mornings and during the week. Daytime and evening classes flex with the various working shifts of those in our congregations. By offering classes in the local church, and where appropriate, in offices and homes, we can move people along the continuum from newborn believers to mature Christians.

Leader's Tip

For an effective teaching ministry in the local church, it is vital to have a clear vision of Christian education. The following purpose and mission statements are examples of the philosophical foundation on which a teaching ministry should build.

The Purpose of a Christian Education Ministry

Purpose

The purpose of Christian education is *transformation teaching*. Our goal is to teach the Word of God so that lives are changed and minds are transformed according to Romans 12:1–2. This education occurs in a stimulating environment where children, youth, and adults learn doctrinal truths at their developmental level.

Mission

The mission of Christian education is embodied in the acrostic *TEACH*:

T rain Leaders
E quip Parents
A ssess and Evaluate Existing Ministries
C hallenge Excellence
H olistically Meet Needs

Train Leaders. Teachers' meetings, special classes, conferences, seminars, Bible school, and seminary are ways to train teachers and volunteers. Teachers of children and teenagers should meet once a month to discuss issues, share ideas and information, and be encouraged.

Equip Parents. Parents are the primary teachers of their children. Reinforcement of Bible lessons and help with Scripture memorization are the responsibility of the home. The church's responsibility is to teach parents to model Christ so that their children may one day own their faith. Parenting seminars are an important way to equip parents.

Assess and Evaluate Existing Ministries. Ministries and leaders should be periodically assessed and evaluated. Above all, they should be encouraged and supported. Visiting other ministries and churches are additional ways to expose leadership to viable ministry models.

Challenge Excellence. In the twenty-first century, we must challenge our Christian education team to strive for excellence. A professional approach, decorum, and presentation are key to remaining on the cutting edge. Educational goals must be in step with tomorrow. We must continue to grow spiritually and professionally, to explore new ideas, and to reject the status quo. We must work for the glory of God.

Holistically Meet Needs. Our task is to minister to the needs of the whole person—educationally, socially, and professionally. In this way, learners experience God's divine care. Even as we care for others, it is our personal task to care for ourselves as well. Modeling godliness is one of the teacher's most effective tools.

Why Do We Teach?

In Christian education, learning is measured by life change. This is more than just the mere soaking up of facts! Learning is a vibrant process that involves a change of mind and heart evidenced by one's behavior. Romans 12:1–2 calls this process *transformation*.

> Therefore, I urge you, brothers, in view of God's mercy, to offer your bodies as living sacrifices, holy and pleasing to God—this is your spiritual act of worship. Do not conform any longer to the pattern of this world, but be transformed by the renewing of your mind. Then you will be able to test and approve what God's will is—his good, pleasing and perfect will.
>
> —ROMANS 12:1–2

The type of teaching that causes transformation occurs when learners replace bad habits with biblical ones, when godly thought processes result in right actions. As teachers, we partner with the Holy Spirit in this transforming process.

Nurturing bench-sitting believers with the Word of God so that they grow beyond the point of mere Sunday morning church attendance builds leaders who will, in turn, teach others also (2 Tim. 2:2). Correcting those who come to our churches with false doctrines and helping those who need exhortation to live holy lives are additional tasks in building up the body of Christ. This is the purpose of the Word of God.

> All Scripture is God-breathed and is useful for teaching, rebuking, correcting and training in righteousness, so that the man of God may be thoroughly equipped for every good work.
>
> —2 TIMOTHY 3:16–17

Not to be overlooked is reaching unbelievers. Evangelism is designed to rescue the perishing. We teach this glorious gospel to answer the doubters and to convince the skeptical.

How Do We Teach?

Jesus, the most effective teacher who ever lived, is our model. By teaching as he taught, we can sharpen our skills and transform our classrooms. As the Master Teacher, Jesus employed methods that embrace every teaching theory and practice. His teaching provides us with insight into the teacher, learner, environment, curriculum, and methodology—areas that we will explore in the next chapter.

A Philosophy of Ministry

When we evaluate who we teach, what we teach, when and where we teach, why we teach, and how we teach, we are defining our philosophy of ministry. This provides the basis for everything we do. The way that we apply each of these aspects in our individual churches and classrooms may vary from culture to culture. In other words, the "what" we teach (the Bible) and the "why" we teach (transformation) are not likely to change. However, the "how" we teach is flexible, depending on the "when" and the "where" we teach and for "whom" we teach the "what" we teach.

African-American, Korean, Ethiopian, Filipino, Latino, Puerto Rican, Chinese, Samoan, Caucasian, and Indian are just a sampling of the wonderful array of cultures who add their own ethnic nuance to the teaching experience. Best of all (as we will see), Jesus encourages us to personalize our lessons by adding a little spice to our teaching. In the next chapter, we will take a closer look at Jesus, the Master Teacher.

Part One

Principles from Jesus

Chapter 2

Jesus, the Master Teacher
Principles of Teaching

Objective

By the end of this chapter, you will evaluate the importance of five major areas in the teaching-learning process by examining the teaching principles modeled by Jesus, the Master Teacher.

He never sat in a classroom. He never went to college. He never learned a degree. Yet Jesus is unquestionably the greatest teacher who ever lived. Whenever he taught, multitudes followed. With three short years to complete his task, the Master Teacher ministered with focus and purpose.

Modeling the Master

Why was Jesus considered the Master Teacher? What methods did he model to help us become more effective teachers? How can we take the truths from the Word of God and teach them in refreshingly new, exciting, and memorable ways? Can we teach so that the Bible is relevant today both in the city as well as in the suburb?

There is good news! Jesus did what he did and knew what he knew instinctively. We, however, have to learn effective teaching principles intentionally. By analyzing some major principles embodied in the teachings of Jesus, we will be better equipped to follow in his steps.

1. Jesus Taught Based on His Character

Jesus taught based on his character. Who he was—God Incarnate—was the basis from which he taught. All that he modeled to the disciples and demonstrated to the crowds and religious leaders centered on the fact that he was the Son of God.

For example, as the sinless one, Jesus taught forgiveness (Luke 7:36–50). As King, Jesus taught about the kingdom (Matt. 13). As the living Word, Jesus corrected false teachings (Matt. 15:1–20). He ministered out of love because he is love.

Who are we by nature? As Christian teachers, are we becoming more like Christ? In the process of making disciples, we must closely follow the Lord so that learners see him in our character. Laboring with integrity, teaching with honest hearts, correcting others with pure motives, and receiving correction with right attitudes are the marks of a "discipler" of disciples. The teacher's Christian character is key, and we will discuss this in-depth in the next chapter.

2. Jesus Understood the Learner

Jesus, the Master Teacher, understood the learner. Much of what we call teaching today has shifted the focus from the personal needs of the learner to the personality preferences of the teacher. As Jesus demonstrated, it should be quite the reverse. The needs of the student determine what is to be taught.

Little Zacchaeus, who climbed up the sycamore tree to get a glimpse of Jesus, was converted because Jesus understood that Zacchaeus needed his attention (Luke 19:1). This chief tax collector had illegally benefited from his profession and was among the despised of his day. Still, he wanted to see Jesus, so he decided to go up higher for a better view.

While passing by, Jesus looked up at Zacchaeus in the tree, called him by name, and told him to come down. That day Jesus would be a guest in Zacchaeus's home. Before the visit ended, Zacchaeus was a changed man who had promised to repay four times the original amount to everyone whom he had cheated.

What did Jesus do first? He established relationship. By identifying with the learner he was able to effect change in his behavior.

Do we take the time to establish relationships with our students? Sometimes just looking in their direction and noticing them as people is enough to turn a life around. Spending time with students outside of the classroom in appropriate settings, talking with them about their education, careers, and professions demonstrates that we see them as real people with real needs. As we will see later in this book, visiting students where they are—for example, junior high and high school students in their schools—adds a personal touch to any educational ministry.

3. Jesus Taught Developmentally

Jesus taught each age group in keeping with its developmental level. Contrary to the disciples' practices, Jesus made time for children and considered them very important. He allowed them to participate in his ministry. By using a little boy's lunch, Jesus fed five thousand men, plus women and children (John 6:9–13).

At every age—from preschool children to senior citizens—learners have specific needs that our teaching must address. The ability of the learner to understand what we are teaching must be taken into account. Therefore, we must tailor our teaching so that it is age-appropriate and applicable to their needs. We will look more closely at development when we discuss how to teach at every age level in Part 2.

4. Jesus Used Teachable Moments

Jesus was the master of teachable moments! His goal was to capitalize on the students' readiness to learn. For example, a storm and the fear of perishing was a perfect time for Jesus to teach his disciples to have faith in him (Matt. 14:31). When the disciples were humbled by their failure to heal, Jesus used this opportune time to teach them about the importance of power through prayer (Mark 9:29). And when the disciples wanted to learn how to pray, Jesus taught them (Luke 11:1).

At a teachable moment, students are eager to acquire information that helps them answer questions, meet requirements, or cope with their situations. Readiness to learn is often dependent on life events—baptism, marriage, birth of a child—that are particularly significant in the experience of the learner.

Like Jesus, teachable moments also demand readiness on the part of the teacher. Jesus prayed during his most difficult hours, modeling how to successfully handle a crisis (John 17). Even in the shadow of the cross, Jesus taught. By being alert to teachable moments, we, too, can motivate students to learn what they need to learn. Much of this education occurs through the day-to-day examples we model when coping with our own life experiences.

The Christian teacher must be attentive so that the teachable moment is not lost. When we study the adult learner, we'll discuss more about how to maximize teachable moments.

5. Jesus Was Sensitive to Time

Throughout his ministry, Jesus was sensitive to time. He was aware of the beginning, middle, and end of his ministry, time of day, and day of the week.

Jesus began his ministry by performing a miracle at the wedding in Cana (John 2:1–11). His purpose was to reveal his glory so that his disciples would be encouraged to put their faith in him (v. 11). The timing of this miracle was essential.

Jesus healed the man who was born blind to shine the spotlight on the spiritual blindness of the Pharisees who refused to recognize him as Messiah (9:1–41). He raised Lazarus from the dead before his private ministry to the disciples (11:54) and prior to the anointing in preparation for his own burial (12:1–7). After raising Lazarus, Jesus stressed his own death and resurrection.

The Lord healed the paralytic when "the power of the Lord was present for him to heal the sick" (Luke 5:17–25). He chose the time of the Sabbath to heal the man with the withered hand to teach that "doing good" on the Sabbath was the fulfillment of the law (6:6–10).

In another example, Jesus chose the early morning hours to walk on the water when and where only the disciples could see him (Mark 6:48–52). At the appointed time, Jesus sent the disciples to preach and heal (6:7–13). Aware that they were tired when they returned, Jesus took them to a quiet place to rest (6:31). At a different time, when the crowds skipped their lunch to listen to Jesus, he recognized that it was time to eat, and he fed them (Luke 9:10–17).

When it comes to our lesson planning, we can learn from this principle of sequencing—placing our lessons in a specific order just as Jesus did to correspond with the beginning, middle, and end of his ministry. His lessons built on what the disciples had previously learned. Sequencing—what comes first, what comes next, and what comes last—is part of the curriculum development process and is discussed in chapter 6, "Pray . . . Plan . . . Prepare."

6. Jesus Capitalized on the Environment

Jesus used his environment to maximize every teaching opportunity. He taught in homes and on boats, in mountains and in deserts, at weddings and at funeral processions. His teachings were never confined to one place or building. Jesus knew that the majority of students were outside rather than within synagogue walls.

For the Master Teacher, environment was crucial to the lesson. Imagine the Sermon on the Mount. As Jesus sat on the mountainside, he probably pointed to the birds and flowers around him when he said, "Look at the birds of the air; . . . See how the lilies of the field grow" (Matt. 6:26–28).

Remember the teaching episode that occurred at the retreat in Caesarea Philippi? On the boat leaving Galilee, prior to arriving at Caesarea Philippi, Jesus had warned the disciples about the leaven of the Pharisees and Sadducees (Matt. 16:6). Misunderstanding his statement, the disciples remarked that they had forgotten to bring bread. Jesus corrected them by reminding them of the miracles in feeding the multitudes (16:8–10). Then he said, "Do you have eyes but fail to see, and ears but fail to hear?" (Mark 8:18).

With this exhortation for spiritual perception, the disciples were alert and eager to avoid another reprimand from their teacher. Finally, they arrived at Caesarea Philippi, a lush and verdant area with beautiful waterfalls and dangling vines—the perfect setting for reflection and meditation. Here they were intent to focus on spiritual matters rather than on fleshly concerns. And they were unlikely to miss the point this time.

> When Jesus came to the region of Caesarea Philippi, he asked his disciples, "Who do people say the Son of Man is?"
> They replied, "Some say John the Baptist; others say Elijah; and still others, Jeremiah or one of the prophets."
> "But what about you?" he asked. "Who do you say I am?"
> Simon Peter answered, "You are the Christ, the Son of the living God."
>
> —MATTHEW 16:13–16

Peter, the spokesperson, answered on behalf of the disciples, and his confession mirrored the heartbeat of the group. Jesus had taken his students to this quiet resort area precisely for this purpose—to reflect on all they had seen, heard, and experienced.

Likewise, we must capitalize on the environment whenever we teach. Whether in homes, school buildings, church auditoriums, recreation areas, or at conference sites, the setting where we teach is an important factor in the teaching-learning process. Settings determine the methods we will be able to use. Basics such as overheads and desks, or having students sit on the floor, for example, are determined by the setting. Because each environment is different, the way we teach must change accordingly.

7. Jesus Considered Cultural Needs

The Master Teacher was always in touch with the culture of his students. His teachings were sprinkled with examples and anecdotes from the Jewish culture, his primary audience. Because they were an agrarian people, Jesus used similes and metaphors that involved farming, harvesting, and shepherding:

By their fruit you will recognize them.

—MATTHEW 7:16

The harvest is plentiful but the workers are few.

—MATTHEW 9:37

If a man owns a hundred sheep, and one of them wanders away, will he not leave the ninety-nine on the hills and go to look for the one that wandered off?

—MATTHEW 18:12

Cookie-cutter classes don't work. We can't take material from one culture and overlay it onto another culture and expect to teach effectively. We must tailor our teaching to the needs and experiences of our target audience.

The Synoptic Gospels are an excellent example of this principle. In retelling the account of Jesus, each writer relates to the background of his audience. Matthew's gospel, written to the Jews, is an apologetic for Jesus as Messiah. It traces the lineage of Christ as the Son of David, the Son of Abraham, and therefore Israel's legal king (Matt. 1:1). Mark writes to the Romans who were a people of action, and the author quickly moves us from one event to another with the frequent use of the word "immediately." Writing primarily to a Greek audience, Luke stirs the emotion with his portraits of Jesus responding to the despised and downtrodden.

As we teach in the local church, the Bible is our primary curriculum. And it *is* culturally relevant! Biblical history occurred in the Middle East, in Africa, and in Asia. Jesus hid for three years in Egypt on the continent of Africa and the prophecy, "Out of Egypt I called my son," was fulfilled (see Matt. 2:13–15).

Several books already on the market underscore the rich variety of cultures couched in biblical heritage. Care must be exercised to avoid extremes. As my pastor explains, the Bible is neither "Afrocentric" nor "Eurocentric." It is "bibliocentric." On the other hand, ignoring facts that are inclusive of people of color is inconsistent with the integrity of the text. Sound Bible study methods demonstrate that God loves everyone, and in keeping with his nature, his Word is inclusive.

Our secondary curriculum choices—the printed materials we purchase in bookstores or order from publishing houses—help us determine whether we are addressing the cultural needs of our learners. Some publishing houses specialize in developing materials for a particular ethnic market. Where curriculum misses the mark, writing and developing our own is essential. To assist in the evaluation of the material you are using, a "Curriculum Evaluation Checklist" is included near the end of chapter 6, "Pray . . . Plan . . . Prepare."

8. Jesus Appealed to the Mind, Emotions, and Behavior

Jesus taught so that the learner would be changed. To accomplish this, he appealed to every aspect of the learner's decision-making process—the mind (cognitive domain), the emotions (affective domain), and the behavior (psychomotor domain).

His parables appealed to the learner's ability to think and reason—the cognitive domain. For instance, a sinful woman appeared at Simon's house with an alabaster jar of perfume. She kissed his feet and wiped them with her tears and hair. Knowing the Pharisees' thoughts, Jesus told the parable of two men who owed money to a lender. One owed a great amount, and the other a small amount.

> "Neither of them had the money to pay him back, so he canceled the debts of both. Now which of them will love him the more?"
>
> Simon replied, "I suppose the one who had the bigger debt canceled."
>
> "You have judged correctly," Jesus said.
>
> Then he turned toward the woman and said to Simon, "Do you see this woman? I came into your house. You did not give me any water for my feet, but she wet my feet with her tears and wiped them with her hair. You did not give me a kiss, but this woman, from the time I entered, has not stopped kissing my feet. You did not put oil on my head, but she has poured perfume on my feet. Therefore, I tell you, her many sins have been forgiven—for she loved much. But he who has been forgiven little loves little."
>
> —LUKE 7:42–47

Jesus also addressed the affective domain where feelings are paramount. During an emotional rivalry debate among the disciples, Jesus settled the issue by explaining that in order to be great in the kingdom, one must be humble like a little child (Matt. 18:1; Mark 9:35;

Luke 9:46). Another emotional incident occurred when the disciples witnessed righteous zeal in action as Jesus angrily cleansed the temple (Mark 11:15).

Commissioning the disciples to preach, to cast out demons, and to anoint with oil and heal the sick (Mark 6:7–13) illustrates how the Master Teacher encouraged the disciples in their actions—the psychomotor domain. By putting into practice what they had learned, they became active participants in his ministry.

We can decide in advance what the student will know, feel, and do. Having a clear understanding of what we are going to teach and how we are going to teach it helps us to address the cognitive, affective, and psychomotor domains. Note the examples given throughout this book.

9. Jesus Involved the Senses

Perhaps the principle that is most intriguing is how Jesus reinforced his teachings by involving all of the senses: he *touched* people; they *listened* to him; they *saw* his miracles.

Mary's anointing of Jesus for his burial sparked a teaching session (Matt. 26:6–13; Mark 14: 3–9; John 12:2–11). Here the disciples saw the anointing (visual), smelled the perfume (olfactory), and heard the prophecy (auditory). In Matthew 12, the disciples were hungry and they ate the grain (kinesthetic), an experience that Jesus used later in his teaching on the Sabbath (Matt. 12:1–8). Visually, Peter, James, and John saw the transfiguration (Matt. 17:1–13). The cross, painted for us through the eyes of the gospel writers, is perhaps the most powerful visual of them all!

As Christian teachers, we may be too content to limit ourselves to one learning channel—auditory. The teacher who realizes that we learn through all of our senses—visual (seeing), auditory (hearing), kinesthetic (doing)—will be the most effective and the most creative. Understanding how we prefer to learn, which is called learning channels, is key to this process. We will explore learning channels in chapter 4, "Through the Learner's Lens."

10. Jesus Addressed Social Concerns

Jesus went out of his way to teach the Samaritan woman at the well in the context of her social condition (John 4:4). He was aware of her status in the community, a woman who, because of her adulterous life, dared not draw water during the early morning hours along with the respectable women. Instead, she came at noon during the heat of the day when everyone else was inside, cooled by the shade.

At the well, understanding her social predicament, the Teacher met the Samaritan woman at her point of need. She was drawing fresh water yet dying of spiritual thirst—a slave to satisfying her flesh when the fulfillment she needed could only come from God. Using water metaphors, Jesus introduced her to his revitalizing, thirst-quenching power.

For us, the key to successful ministry in the local church is to teach within the context of social needs. We must consider our students' culture and ethnicity when planning our lessons. And by allowing students to openly respond, to discuss issues from their point of view, and even to disagree, we underscore that we value their perspective and demonstrate our respect for them.

Time for a Test

In this overview, we have examined 10 important teaching principles from the Master Teacher. Can you recall each of the points discussed in this chapter?

Principles from Jesus, Master Teacher

1. Jesus taught based on _____.

2. Jesus understood the _____.

3. Jesus taught _____.

4. Jesus used _____.

5. Jesus was _____.

6. Jesus capitalized _____.

7. Jesus considered _____.

8. Jesus appealed to _____.

9. Jesus involved _____.

10. Jesus addressed _____.

Leader's Tip

Give your students the handout on the previous page and ask them to complete the sentences as you read and explain the answers. Using the Gospels as their source, ask students to offer their own examples of each teaching principle.

The following outline summarizes what we have learned. As we look at these points, they may be divided into five categories:

A. The Teacher

    1. Jesus taught based on his character.
    2. Jesus understood the learner.

B. The Learner

    1. Jesus taught developmentally.
    2. Jesus used teachable moments.

C. Time and Environment

    1. Jesus was sensitive to time.
    2. Jesus capitalized on the environment.

D. The Curriculum

    1. Jesus considered cultural needs.
    2. Jesus appealed to mind, emotions, and behavior.

E. Methodology

    1. Jesus involved the senses.
    2. Jesus addressed social concerns.

The Teaching Hand

Using a "Teaching Hand" on the following page as a model, let's overlay these areas to get a picture of the important areas in effective teaching.

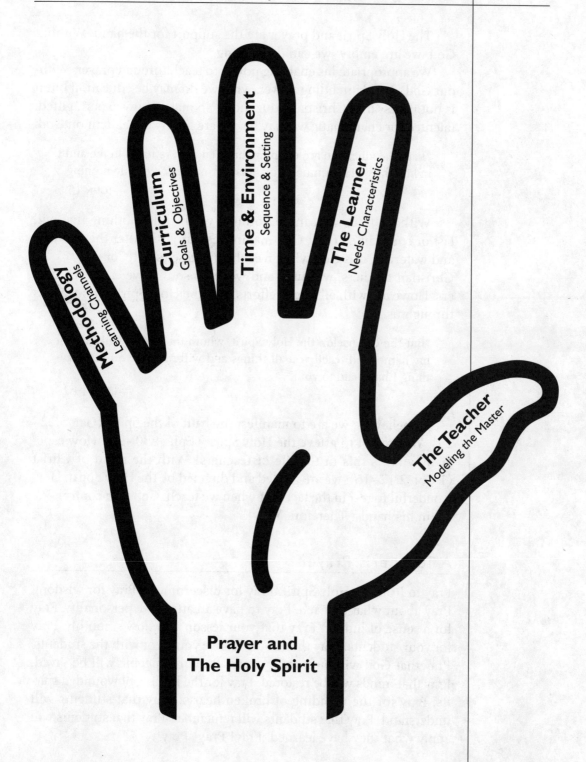

Methodology
Learning Channels

Curriculum
Goals & Objectives

Time & Environment
Sequence & Setting

The Learner
Needs Characteristics

The Teacher
Modeling the Master

**Prayer and
The Holy Spirit**

The Holy Spirit and prayer are the support for the hand. Without God, we are empty; we can do nothing.

We appropriate his enabling power to teach through prayer. Without God's superintending power, what we do may be education but it is not necessarily Christian education. No matter how expert, gifted, talented, or charismatic we may be, we are totally dependent on God.

> "I am the vine; you are the branches. If a man remains in me and I
> in him, he will bear much fruit; apart from me you can do nothing."
>
> —JOHN 15:5

Without Jesus we can do nothing worthwhile, nothing that will last or count in eternity. God maximizes our gifts. After the planting and watering, it is God who gives the increase (see 1 Cor. 3:6–7). As Christian teachers, we study and we learn so that we can teach others. However, with all of our efforts, it is the Holy Spirit who teaches through us.

> "But the Counselor, the Holy Spirit, whom the Father will send in
> my name, will teach you all things and will remind you of every-
> thing I have said to you."
>
> —JOHN 14:26

As believers, we are to manifest the fruit of the Spirit (Gal. 5:22–25). We are not to grieve the Holy Spirit (Eph. 4:30–32). How especially vital is this in the life of teachers! With the mind of Christ (1 Cor. 2:12–16), we are guided and directed by the Holy Spirit. How wonderful to rest in the fact that when we teach, God is in control. We are in his hands. Therefore, pray!

A Teacher's Prayer

Pray to hear the Holy Spirit. Pray for discernment. Pray for wisdom. Pray about what to teach. Pray to have an attractive personality. Pray for a sense of humor. Pray that your lesson will flow smoothly. Pray for your students. Pray that God will give you favor with the students. Pray that God will meet their needs. Pray that people will be saved. Pray that minds will be restored. Pray for the healing of wounded spirits. Pray for the mending of broken hearts. Pray that students will understand. Pray that students will remember. Pray that students will apply what they have learned. Pray! Pray! Pray!

Do You Remember?

In this chapter we examined principles of teaching illustrated in Jesus' own teaching situations. These ten points divide into five major areas of the teaching-learning process: the teacher, the learner, time and environment, the curriculum, and methodology.

Below is a summary of these 10 major points.

Jesus taught based on his character.	Learners must see Jesus in us.
Jesus understood the learner.	Consider the needs of our students.
Jesus taught developmentally.	Learners have specific needs.
Jesus used teachable moments.	Teachable moments are times when students are eager to acquire information.
Jesus was sensitive to time.	Sequencing is key in curriculum development.
Jesus capitalized on the environment.	The teaching setting is important.
Jesus considered cultural needs.	We must tailor our teaching to the needs and experiences of our learners.
Jesus appealed to mind, emotions, and behavior.	We must address the mind, emotions, and behavior when we teach.
Jesus involved the senses.	We learn through all of our senses—visual (seeing), auditory (hearing), and kinesthetic (doing).
Jesus addressed social concerns.	We must teach within the context of social needs.

A Measure of Success

Success will occur only when we model the Master. But keep in mind that ministry success is not always measured in numbers. Were this true, our Savior's ministry would be considered by some to be a failure. As has often been said, Jesus ended his earthly ministry with a church of only 11 men and a few women. Obviously, success is more than numbers, because these men and women won converts who turned the world upside down (Acts 17:6).

Effective Teaching and Busy Churches

Where effective teaching is taking place, churches are as busy during the week as they are on Sunday mornings, buzzing with people, Bibles in hand. And employing the teaching principles of Jesus is guaranteed to enliven any ministry. Let's begin to explore these principles more in-depth by evaluating the first principle: Jesus taught based on who he was, which involves the teacher's character.

How effective are Christian teachers if they are not people of integrity, people of character? How effective is teaching without being solidly grounded in the Word of God? What about teachers who have the gift of teaching but who do not really love God's people? What kind of a role model is a person who teaches certain biblical truths but doesn't live according to them? Finally, can a teacher be effective without knowing how to teach?

You ask good questions! The answers are in the next chapter.

Chapter 3

Most Memorable Teacher
Teacher's Character and Other Essentials

Objective

By the end of this chapter, you will evaluate the importance of Christian character by deciding on the qualities that are essential for effective teachers.

The Bible has been removed from public schools. Now, teachers and administrators are trying to decide how to give students what they are lacking most—a solid moral foundation. "Character Education," curriculum that teaches students about honesty, truthfulness, respect, self-control, and other virtues essential to successful living, has become the norm.

How important is character in the local church? Have we embraced the outward show of spirituality at the cost of genuine Christian character?

My most memorable teacher was Irene Samuel, a professor of Literary Criticism at New York's Hunter College. She was a brilliant teacher. Since I was attending school during a time of civil unrest—the Vietnam War—I often cut her class to picket and protest. Like every other idealist, I felt obligated to change the world. As a result, my studies suffered.

On a day that I did decide to attend Professor Samuel's class, I sat in the back, daydreaming about the next protest strategy. We had already blocked traffic on Park Avenue, squeezed glue into the keyholes of the administrative offices, sat in classrooms, and refused to move—that is, until the soldiers in tanks arrived! I was somewhere in the middle of designing my next picket sign when Professor Samuel called my name.

"Please answer the question," she said to another student, "because it concerns Miss Powlis." I was jerked back into the reality of Literary Criticism I with the mention of my name. Needless to say,

I panicked. What had I missed? What happened? What question did she just ask?

Fortunately, Professor Samuel did not want me to answer any question. She merely wanted my attention, and she now had it . . . *completely!* She proceeded to chastise me in front of the entire class. She told me that I was wasting my college years. She said I needed to refocus my energies and attend class, that I had talent as a writer and needed to reorder my priorities. Everyone else remained silent as she used the remaining 40 or so minutes to enumerate my shortcomings and challenged me to do better.

Singed with embarrassment, I was also silently elated. Everyone knew that Professor Samuel was one of the most difficult teachers in the entire English Department. This teacher, whom I had thought barely noticed me, said that I had *talent*? It mattered to *her* what I did with my life?

I never cut her class again. I aced her exams. The following semester, Professor Samuel did a slight doubletake and looked with warm approval as I marched into her class for Literary Criticism II.

My Most Memorable Teacher

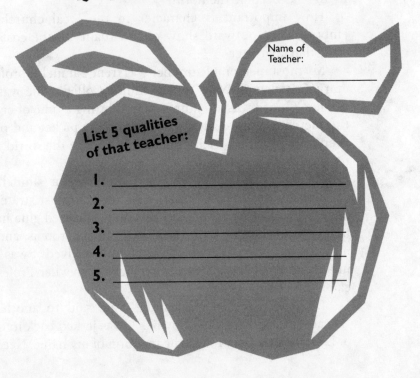

Name of Teacher:

_____

List 5 qualities of that teacher:

1. _____
2. _____
3. _____
4. _____
5. _____

An Indelible Mark

A memorable teacher leaves an indelible mark on our lives. Think about a teacher you can never forget. Sometimes it's because he or she left a negative impression. Still, this teacher is memorable because we vow never to be like that! As you reminisce, perhaps it's a math teacher, a physical education teacher, youth worker, Sunday school teacher, pastor, or Bible study teacher whom you remember most.

In the Teacher's Apple on the previous page, write the name of that teacher in the leaf at the top. In the apple itself, list reasons why this is one teacher you will never forget.

Your list probably included some characteristics like the following:

> Was a good listener
> Prayed for me
> Expected only the best
> Spent time with me
> Encouraged me
> Had a sense of humor
> Went out of the way to help me
> Managed the class well
> Gave correction when needed
> Taught with enthusiasm
> Was very creative
> Administered discipline appropriately
> Was never boring
> Loved teaching
> Cared about me

It is interesting to note what *isn't* on the list. Most teachers aren't remembered because they really knew their math, or because they could recite all of the salient details of the intertestamental period. It is usually the intangible qualities inherent in the strong character of a teacher that leave a lasting impression.

Effective Teachers

Few would argue that the most effective teachers are those who follow their own instruction. Perfection is not required, but for teachers, there is a definite standard. Do we wait until what we teach becomes a discipline in our own lives before we can teach? Or, can we be "in process" as we teach? What if a teaching opportunity presents itself before that process is complete? Can we "talk the talk" before we "walk the walk"?

The Bible does not give teachers an option. Since a teacher teaches by what he or she says *and* does, scriptural guidelines are clear, and the consequence for disobedience is severe.

> Anyone who breaks one of the least of these commandments and teaches others to do the same will be called least in the kingdom of heaven, but whoever practices and teaches these commands will be called great in the kingdom of heaven.
>
> —MATTHEW 5:19

Whenever we interpret Scripture, word order is important. Notice that in the verse above, the word "practice" precedes the word "teaches." Therefore, practice comes first. We are qualified to teach others *only after* we have learned how to personally practice the teachings of Jesus Christ on a daily basis. This order is set by God himself. As teachers, our walk before the Lord must be exemplary. To stay firmly on our feet, we must stay on our knees!

It is essential for prospective teachers to be proven. If new to a church, they need to be observed for at least a year and references need to be checked before they receive any major responsibility. If inappropriate behavior is discovered, the following applies.

> In fact, though by this time you ought to be teachers, you need someone to teach you the elementary truths of God's word all over again. You need milk, not solid food! Anyone who lives on milk, being still an infant, is not acquainted with the teaching about righteousness. But solid food is for the mature, who by constant use have trained themselves to distinguish good from evil.
>
> —HEBREWS 5:12–14

Character Counts

For the Christian educator, character counts! Rather than placing emphasis on whether a teacher really knows the Bible or whether a teacher has charisma, we should begin with the teacher's character. Does the teacher have integrity? Often, as the saying goes, "only time will tell." Observe prospective teachers and pay attention to their reputation.

Now that we've addressed this basic step in evaluating the Christian teacher, we are ready to investigate further. Let's see what a teacher would look like if he or she were missing one of the essential ingredients for effective teaching.

Leader's Tip

Discuss these following statements with the teachers you are training. Prior to class, post an "Agree" sign on one side of the room. On the other, post the "Disagree" sign.

Retype the questions below using a large font size and display them using an overhead projector. Unveil questions one by one. Ask students to get up out of their seats and stand on the side of the room that represents their decision. There can be no middle ground. Everyone must choose one side or the other.

Allow representatives from each side to explain why they agree or disagree. (*Note:* The teacher must remain neutral during this process.) After approximately five minutes of discussion, move on to the next statement.

Agree or Disagree?

To clarify the importance of Christian character, examine the following scenarios. Indicate either "Agree" or "Disagree" by moving to one side of the room.

1. An English professor at a secular school can live an immoral life and still be an effective teacher.

   Agree?   **Disagree?**

2. An adult Bible study teacher can be an effective teacher even though he smokes a cigarette outside church immediately after the service.

   Agree?   **Disagree?**

3. A divorced person, who is a gifted teacher, can still be an effective teacher for the singles ministry.

   Agree?   **Disagree?**

4. The most effective teachers follow their own instruction.

   Agree?   **Disagree?**

"Effective" is the key word in each sentence. In Scenario #1, it may or may not matter whether an English teacher at a secular school lives an immoral life. Students may not respect this teacher, but they may still learn. Whether or not this teacher is *effective,* however, depends on how seriously students are influenced by the immoral lifestyle.

Does the same hold true in the other situations? Let's examine some more.

In Scenario #2, the adult Bible study teacher may have the ability to teach and recruit class members. But what is he modeling, not only to his students, but also to the children and teenagers who see him as a role model in the church? Whether or not smoking is regarded as sinful, it is certainly undesirable due to its negative effect on one's health. So in the exercise of wisdom, smoking should be avoided. At the very least, this teacher might do well to wait and smoke that cigarette at home. He was asked to do so by the Christian education pastor, and he obliged.

In Scenario #3, questions might arise concerning who is at fault for the divorce. Without knowing any background, however, we can still make a decision, even if it is with reservations. Has the teacher submitted to the disciplinary process and counseling of church leadership? Have forgiveness and healing occurred? Here, the key is the process—submission, healing, forgiveness, and restoration. This person must willingly submit to church leadership before being given any responsibility as a teacher. Such was the case in a local church, and now that pastor teaches a weekly gathering of nearly one thousand single people!

Essential Ingredients

Like the well-blended ingredients in a cake, the effective teacher is a balanced combination of essential qualities and skills. Separately, flour is just flour, milk is just milk, butter is just butter, and sugar, though sweet, is not delicious when eaten alone. But mixed together, these ingredients make a mouth-watering delight. If you eliminate even one ingredient—milk, butter, sugar, eggs, or flour—you will have a catastrophe, not a cake!

In the box on the following page are the essential ingredients for an effective teacher—biblical knowledge and accurate interpretation of Scripture, interpersonal rapport, teaching skill, and moral excellence. Together, these ingredients make a well-balanced teacher who is equipped by God, engaged with the learner, exciting as a teacher, and excellent as a role model. The result? The Word of God becomes irresistible, drawing people into our churches, into our classrooms, and most of all, into the loving arms of Jesus Christ.

Biblical Knowledge

What would teachers look like if they were missing biblical knowledge? In other words, what if they could not properly interpret Scripture?

The obvious result is that teachers would be weak in the fundamentals of the faith. Such teachers may be dogmatic, shallow, and legalistic. Worse, however, is the potential for heresy. Teachers who have not been properly taught can be a disaster to any class and a destroyer of any church.

When God calls a man or woman into the field of Christian education, the call is just the beginning. Never allow enthusiasm to overshadow adequate biblical preparation. The greater the teaching responsibility, the higher the requirement for credentials. For example, Paul did not immediately begin teaching after his conversion. Instead, three years of preparation preceded his ministry (Gal. 1:17–18).

Sunday school teachers can be trained within the context of the local church. Those who want to teach youth or adults must have a sound biblical foundation. Mature believers who have personally studied the Scriptures and attended churches with good Bible teaching can be excellent in the classroom. Others may need to attend Bible college or seminary. Whatever the choice, good training is essential.

Lack of money is an unacceptable excuse for not attending school. Although not an actual passage of Scripture, the old saying, "Where God guides, God provides," is still true. If God has called a person to teach, can he not also provide for the tuition? Low-cost student loans are available, and it's worth the investment. Some student loans are

Essential Ingredients for an Effective Teacher

Box A	Box B
Biblical Knowledge and Interpretation of Scripture	Interpersonal Rapport and Concern for the Listener
Box C	**Box D**
Teaching Skill	Moral Excellence

"forgiven" if certain requirements are met. Students with good GPAs can obtain scholarships and grants. In some seminaries, students can even secure jobs on campus to help supplement tuition. Education can be expensive, but God *will* supply every need (Phil. 4:19).

An African-American student was short on funds during one of her final semesters at a Christian university. Afraid that she would have to leave school, she met with the ethnic advisor to share her concern. Together they prayed for a miracle.

A few days later, they learned that the snack shop was being renovated. The decor centered on a 1940s theme and the managers were searching for an old-fashioned juke box to add to the ambiance.

Here was the answer to prayer! Several months earlier, the student had appeared on a television game show and had won a vintage juke box as a prize. She sold hers to the school and was able to pay her tuition for the entire semester.

God always makes a way! And he is so creative. Sometimes he mixes faith with a little perspiration to provide an education.

Ministering to the deaf had become Regina Cromwell's passion, and she realized how important it was to go to college to learn the language. She and her husband were already existing on one salary, so squeezing money for tuition out of the family budget was impossible.

Determined to become proficient in sign language, she took a job with the transit authority—cleaning the busses at night—to pay for her courses. On Sunday mornings, Regina came straight to church after leaving work at 5 A.M. There she would use the skills she was learning to minister to the deaf. Today, Regina is a co-leader of that ministry.

Education is essential for those who want to teach in the ministry full-time. No longer is seminary training a luxury. It is a necessity! Local churches may offer courses through Bible institutes, and in some instances, this education may be sufficient. Whatever the route, studying is a must!

Do your best to present yourself to God as one approved, a work-man who does not need to be ashamed and who correctly handles the word of truth.

—2 Timothy 2:15

"Correctly handle" means to "cut in a straight direction." An accurate explanation of biblical passages is based on sound hermeneutics—proper Bible study methods. We need to know doctrine, understand the organization of the Bible, know background and historical facts, be aware of authorship and setting, and be skilled in inductive techniques such as observation, interpretation, correlation, and application.

Our entire society is becoming more and more educated. This is also true of people who are attending our churches today. As a result, they are demanding more from their churches, as well they should. Providing Christian educators who are trained to accurately handle the Word of God is the least that we can do.

Leader's Tip

To better equip the teachers in your church, you may want to establish a *Teacher's College*. Tailor the educational format to fit the needs of your staff. One option is to purchase ready-to-use curriculum from the Evangelical Training Association. Contact them at the address below:

Evangelical Training Association
P.O. Box 327
Wheaton, Illinois 60189-0327
(630) 668-6400

For all adult studies, prospective teachers to submit a resumé—teaching is a privilege, isn't it?—and list on it the classes they've completed. If there is only one qualified teacher who can teach your curriculum, then offer one class each semester. Remember, it is irresponsible to appoint teachers who are ill-equipped in teaching the Word of God. It's better to go without that extra Bible class than to have a teacher who is unprepared. God knows the need, and he will send a qualified teacher. Until then, teach the class yourself . . . or wait.

Interpersonal Rapport

Have you ever met a great Bible teacher only to be utterly disappointed when the time came for personal interaction? Is it possible to love teaching but loathe the people?

Teachers who are always irritable when interacting with students may have missed their calling. As my pastor reminded his staff, "We are in the people business. If you don't like people, then I suggest that you do something else!"

A teacher who lacks interpersonal rapport is unapproachable. After class, students may be uncomfortable asking questions or getting additional information when a teacher is insensitive and moody. This teacher offers no encouragement and may simply be incapable of relating to students as individuals. The result? A distant, aloof persona may make it difficult for students to see the personal application of scriptural principles in this teacher's life.

Jesus cared about people and showed compassion for them.

> When he saw the crowds, he had compassion on them, because they were harassed and helpless, like sheep without a shepherd.
>
> —MATTHEW 9:36

Jesus ministered out of love, and that love led him to the ultimate sacrifice—his death on the cross.

We, too, must love the people we teach. Because of the myriad issues plaguing us today, cultivating interpersonal skills is vital in developing a successful teaching ministry. Most people are not looking for a Band-Aid or a handout. What they do need is a listening ear, an empathetic hug that says, "I understand." Being judgmental, impatient, and critical will drive people away rather than attract them to Jesus.

Concern for the learner means that we know how to listen to a person's heart. We are keen observers of nonverbal communication. We learn how to hear what's *not* said as well as what *is* said. And when asked to pray, we stop right then and there and take the extra minute or so to intercede for that person's need. A little attention goes a long way, as we can see in the powerful example that follows.

My home church is located in the core of Koreatown in the central city of Buenos Aires, Argentina. Here, Koreans feel more comfortable speaking Spanish, but they are able to communicate quite freely with their friends in Korean.

When I was seven years old, I immigrated to Argentina with my family. I was mainly educated by the Argentinean system of education, which I do not like so much. Schools and universities close their doors because there is not enough financial support from the government. Teachers are not paid well.

Students do not show much interest since graduating from a university does not guarantee a job in their future. And professors frequently reject Asian youth because they are Koreans. In some schools, students are laughed at by other students and called names like "Chinito," which means Chinese.

When I entered the university, I was totally lost. I had a good GPA, but I did not know what to do with my future. I studied because of my father, but I had problems. Although my attendance at church and in the youth group was perfect, I was spiritually dead.

One day, my youth teacher came to me and said, "Moses, do you know that I am praying for you? God loves you, and I love you, too!" She knew that I was having problems with myself. She knew that I was having problems with my future.

After that short conversation, I began to change. That warm dialogue was the starting point of my commitment to Jesus Christ as his servant. Today, that teacher is still my teacher. I love her very much. She not only helped me out of that difficult situation, but she is currently helping me both spiritually and financially (with tuition expenses in America). I know that even now, she is praying for me. I really thank God for bringing this kind of teacher into my life.

This is the kind of teacher that I want to be. Simple intellectual teaching is not enough. Students need our love. They need our attention. They need our prayers. They need to be listened to. They need to know that God has a plan for their lives. Knowing the real situation of my students, I want to be like my former youth teacher. I believe that this is the only way to teach effectively.

How blessed is this teacher to have borne such fruit through her encouragement of Moses! Today he trains pastors and teachers, and in one seminar alone, Moses taught as many as 150 Korean pastors.

While we struggle in an ever-changing society to keep in step with the needs of those we serve, one fact remains certain. People are the focus of our ministry, the object of our message.

Teaching Skill

Imagine that a teacher has excellent biblical knowledge and strong interpersonal skills, but does not know *how* to teach. How excruciatingly painful for students! In Christian education, the "Eleventh Commandment" is "Thou shalt not bore!"

It is not enough to be knowledgeable about doctrine. Nor is it enough to love God's people. We must also have the ability to communicate what the Bible says. Teaching is a spiritual gift (1 Cor. 12:28; Eph. 4:11), the God-given ability to impart biblical truth in such a way that it is understandable. We teach because we must—even if it means teaching only one student at a time!

I had prepared a church seminar on worship. This was my first time teaching in my new job at the church, and I promised God that if only one student attended, I would teach.

God honored my prayer. He sent *one* student, Sister Mamie Shelton. She attended the entire four weeks, and I taught as I would have for an entire class, with handouts and overheads.

What an incredible time we had singing and studying about worship! The Holy Spirit's presence was tangible. He illumined his Word to us, and we marveled at what we both learned in the process.

Next I decided to tackle Tuesday night Bible study, which had dwindled to a handful of students with the previous teacher. I expected only a few students to attend, but the first night the room was nearly full! Shortly afterwards, we had so many students that we had to use the overflow room.

Was this an example of being faithful over little? That's hard to answer, but God does test the motives of the teacher.

Talking is not *teaching*. Skill in the teaching-learning process involves having clearly defined objectives, understanding age-appropriate teaching, varying methods to adapt to students' learning styles, having smooth transitions from one point to the next, employing the art of storytelling, having strong voice projection, possessing overall teacher presence or charisma, understanding the needs of the learners, and teaching with enthusiasm.

Some of these skills can be taught—others caught. Yes, some aspects of teaching can be learned through observation, but it takes the anointing of the Holy Spirit to blend all of the ingredients to produce an effective teacher.

Jesus is our model. In the discourse of Matthew 13, he demonstrates the value of varying teaching methodology for the benefit of the learner.

> "Have you understood all these things?" Jesus asked. "Yes," they replied.
> He said to them, "Therefore every teacher of the law who has been instructed about the kingdom of heaven is like the owner of a house who brings out of his storeroom new treasures as well as old."
> —MATTHEW 13:51–52

In this chapter Jesus had told a series of parables to explain the kingdom of heaven. The disciples were perplexed at first, but by the seventh parable when the teacher asked if they understood, they heartily replied, "Yes" (Matt. 13:51). Jesus concluded this long discourse by advising every teacher to be like the owner of a house. Within the storeroom are new and old treasures—methods of teaching that help the learner understand.

What's in your storeroom? Examples, stories, sayings, illustrations, and word pictures are different teaching methods that are treasures hidden within the storeroom of our life experiences. They are shaped and colored by our ethnicity and culture and are as varied as are teachers themselves. Our background, childhood, country of origin, and family life provide a wealth of illustrations. These are our own personal treasures.

Regardless of the audience, the teacher's persona ought to shine through. Usually, teaching disasters occur when one teacher tries to teach like someone else. Being ourselves—the unique individuals that God intended with our own histories, recollections, and ways of expression—enriches those to whom we speak.

Perfect that style and stand tall with confidence. Remember, Jesus rarely used the same method twice. The Creator of the universe laced his teachings with variety. To be stuck teaching the same way time and again is, well, to be stuck. In the next chapter, we will discuss how to enliven your lessons by varying your methods.

Moral Excellence

We have come full circle, to the heart of this chapter. The memorable teacher, the teacher with character, reflects moral excellence. The Bible calls moral excellence "holiness."

Holiness is not an option. The teacher who has biblical knowledge, interpersonal rapport, and teaching skill but lacks moral excellence is handling the Word of God deceitfully (2 Cor. 4:2). This teacher is double-minded (James 1:8), has a form of godliness that denies God's power (2 Tim. 3:1–5), and is storing up God's wrath and impending judgment (Rom. 2:5–11). Such a teacher is a poor role model who may lead students to disobey God. For such a person, the Bible poses this rhetorical question:

You, then, who teach others, do you not teach yourself?

—ROMANS 2:21

A shabby lifestyle makes for a shameful teacher who causes others to stumble. Such a teacher has only one choice—sit down.

Do You Remember?

In this chapter, we discussed the qualities essential for effective teachers. Here is a summary of major points to remember:

- *Biblical Knowledge and Interpretation of Scripture.* We may need to attend school to acquire adequate biblical training.
- *Interpersonal Rapport.* We must love the people we teach.
- *Teaching Skill.* We must know how to teach and vary our methodology.
- *Moral Excellence.* Character counts. Holiness is not an option.

The Model Teacher

Jesus, the model teacher, was compassionate, available, and effective. Because he possessed every quality of an effective teacher—knowledge of the Scriptures, interpersonal rapport, teaching skill, and moral excellence—students were either converted or convicted. Oh, to be like Jesus! It's a prayer worth praying!

Now that we have a clearer understanding of what it takes to be an effective teacher, it's time to change our focus and study the learner, which we will do for the remainder of this book. Once we know *how* our students learn, we hold the key to *helping* them learn. Are you ready to take the next step?

Chapter 4

Through the Learner's Lens
Understanding Learning Channels

Objective

By the end of this chapter, you will evaluate the necessity of understanding the learner by comparing learning channels as a way to vary methods for showing, telling, and doing.

J esus taught as if looking through the learner's lens. Insight into the heart of his students helped him to see the world from their point of view so that he could address them at the point of their greatest need. Aware of how people perceive information, Jesus taught by *showing, telling,* and *doing.*

We Learn by Different Means

Isn't it amazing how different we are from culture to culture, ethnic group to ethnic group? We prefer different foods and spices, and we relate to our own style of music. In our own culture, we may have similar facial features and hair textures, but as individuals we are each very different.

There may be two Latino Christians, for example, who share common heritage and language. Although they may have cultural similarities, they may have distinct preferences in worship styles. One may prefer a quiet solemn service while the other may prefer upbeat exuberant celebration.

It is no surprise then that although we may be similar in many respects, we are each different in the way we learn. Each of us has a *learning channel*—the most effective way for us to acquire information. There are three major channels—*seeing, hearing,* and *doing.* Jesus was a master at using teaching methods that targeted each of these channels.

Jesus Taught Through "Seeing"

On the Mount of Transfiguration, Peter, James, and John *saw* Jesus talking with Moses and Elijah (Matt. 17:1–13). So in awe were they that Peter wanted to permanently mark the spot. But establishing a memorial was not the purpose of this lesson. For these three, Jesus allowed them to "see" to further reveal his deity and to unveil his eternality.

In another teaching episode close to the time of Jesus' sacrificial death, Philip asked Jesus to "show us the Father." Jesus answered, "Anyone who has seen me has seen the Father" (John 14:8–9). What a visual for the disciples—and for us! God loves us so much that he sent Jesus for the world to see, and in seeing him, we see the Father!

As witnesses to the miracles—from feeding the multitudes to walking on the water to healing the infirm—the disciples were also learning through seeing. Their most powerful visual lesson, of course, was to see their risen Savior.

Learning is effective when people are involved in *seeing*. The effective teacher must utilize materials that take advantage of this channel. Handouts, pictures, or overhead transparencies are excellent ways to teach those who learn through this *visual* channel. Multimedia, movie clips, television, and computers are additional visual learning tools.

Since what they see is so important, visual learners are very conscious of their physical environment. Neat, attractive classrooms help them to feel comfortable. More than a third of all learners are visual.

Jesus Taught Through "Hearing"

While still in awe at the sight on the Mount of Transfiguration, Peter, James, and John *heard* a voice from the cloud say,

> "This is my Son, whom I love; with him I am well pleased. Listen to him!"
> When the disciples heard this, they fell face down to the ground, terrified. But Jesus came and touched them. "Get up," he said. "Don't be afraid."
>
> —MATTHEW 17:5–7

Needless to say, *hearing* the Father speak from the cloud had to be an astounding auditory experience. And hearing is a powerful way that the disciples learned. While Jesus told parables to the multitudes, it was to the disciples that he explained their meaning.

With many similar parables Jesus spoke the word to them, as much
as they could understand. He did not say anything to them without
using a parable. But when he was alone with his own disciples, he
explained everything.

—MARK 4:33–34

By *hearing* these word pictures, the disciples as learners were able
to identify with the story. Once they understood on a practical level,
it was easier for them to grasp the spiritual concept.

Learning is effective when people are involved in *hearing*. Stories,
lecture, question-and-answer, and audio tapes are just a few examples
of ways to help people learn through the *auditory* channel.

Since auditory learners prefer to use their voices, it is also important for them to speak during the teaching-learning process. Others
may consider them rude when they interrupt the teacher to make
their point, but these learners are actively engaged in acquiring information when they hear their own voices. Neighbor nudge, where two
people are given a certain amount of time to discuss a point, and
small-group discussion are good auditory methods for these learners.

Repeating words helps the auditory learner understand and memorize material. To internalize concepts, these students may read aloud
or mumble to themselves. Auditory learners enjoy sound in their
world, so they can have both the radio and television turned on at the
same time and still learn! However, because they are so sensitive to
sound, unwelcome noise can easily distract. Of all learners, nearly
one-third is auditory.

Jesus Taught Through "Doing"

The multitudes were so intrigued with Jesus that they skipped lunch
to follow him. Concerned, Jesus twice fed thousands with a few loaves
of bread and some fish (Matt. 14:13–21; 15:32–38; Mark 8:1–9; Luke
9:10–17). Though the food was for the multitudes, this lesson was
primarily for the disciples. Jesus involved his learners by having them
do the work of serving the fish and bread. When they collected the
leftovers, they could see the full extent of this miracle up close, but
they failed to understand its significance (Mark 8:17–21).

After gently chastising them, Jesus employed another demonstration perhaps to underscore to his students that clarity of perception for them occurred in stages. He spit on the eyes of a blind man
and laid his hands on him. At first the blind man could see, but like
the disciples, he couldn't see clearly.

"I see people; they look like trees walking around" (Mark 8:24). Only after the second laying on of hands did the blind man see clearly (8:22–26). Like this blind man, it took repeated demonstrations for the disciples to learn the object of their lessons. The Teacher did all that he could to involve his learners and open their eyes.

The Upper Room Discourse provides another example of how Jesus employed *doing* as a teaching method. Upon entering a home, it was the servant's duty, according to custom, to wash the dust from the feet of the guests. None of the disciples had volunteered to take this role, not even to wash Jesus' feet. Jesus got up, tied a towel around his waist, and filled a basin with water. One by one, he began to wash the disciples' feet and dry them with the towel.

> When he had finished washing their feet, he put on his clothes and returned to his place. "Do you understand what I have done for you?" he asked them. "You call me 'Teacher' and 'Lord,' and rightly so, for that is what I am. Now that I, your Lord and Teacher, have washed your feet, you also should wash one another's feet. I have set you an example that you should do as I have done for you."
>
> —JOHN 13:12–15

Imagine their embarrassment! No wonder Peter protested!

Had Jesus given them a lecture, they might have responded by jumping over one another fighting about who would be the first to get the basin, water, and towel, and they would have missed the point entirely. By involving the learners, the Master Teacher was assured that this would be a lesson they would never forget.

Learning is effective when people are involved in *doing*. Those who learn through this *kinesthetic* channel prefer to be physically involved in the lesson. Touching objects, eating, making or building things, working on projects, and even taking notes are all kinesthetic activities.

These learners love to be active. In fact, when in a classroom, they have a difficult time sitting still. They will find an excuse—any excuse—to move from their seat. Learning methods that engage them in the process help to focus their attention. Nearly one-third of all learners are kinesthetic.

Combining Channels

In many instances, Jesus combined the learning channels to reinforce his lessons. He did not simply repeat or restate the message verbally.

He may have used the visual channel (such as writing on the ground) along with the auditory channel (a lecture). Or he may have combined a miracle that everyone could see (visual) with explaining the purpose of the miracle (auditory). Here are a few examples.

Remember the woman who was caught in adultery (John 8:3–11)? The Pharisees, hoping to trap Jesus, dragged her before him demanding that she be stoned. Jesus bent down and wrote on the ground then stood and said:

> "If any one of you is without sin, let him be the first to throw a stone at her."
>
> —JOHN 8:7

We do not know what Jesus wrote, but of this we are certain. Her accusers *saw* what Jesus wrote. And, they *heard* his challenge. Realizing that they too deserved to be stoned, one by one the men left until Jesus was standing alone with the frightened woman.

> Jesus straightened up and asked her, "Woman, where are they? Has no one condemned you?"
>
> "No one, sir," she said.
>
> "Then neither do I condemn you," Jesus declared. "Go now and leave your life of sin."
>
> —JOHN 8:10–11

What a powerful lesson for everyone!

In a different example, Jesus first used the *auditory* channel by announcing, "I am the light of the world" (John 8:12). Then, to reinforce his statement, he offered this *visual* demonstration with the healing of a blind man (9:1). At the end of this teaching episode, the Master Teacher offered this *verbal* summary:

> "For judgment I have come into this world, so that the blind will see and those who see will become blind."
>
> —JOHN 9:39

The Gospels are full of such teaching episodes, but here are two final examples. The first concerns Jesus raising Lazarus from the dead. The second example is Communion.

When her brother, Lazarus, died, Martha was distraught because she felt that Jesus was unconcerned. Knowing his purpose in allowing this to occur, Jesus *says* and *asks* the following:

"I am the resurrection and the life. He who believes in me will live, even though he dies; and whoever lives and believes in me will never die. Do you believe this?"

—JOHN 11:25

Afterward Jesus summoned Mary and went to the tomb. Filled with the pain that death brings, Jesus wept. His critics, noticing the tears, wondered why he had not done something—anything—to prevent this tragedy. Surely, he had the power, the ability. Then why let Lazarus die?

Jesus explained that this death was to glorify God. How? It painted a *visual* picture of the hope of our salvation—the resurrection. Then, Jesus called Lazarus from his tomb. Everyone present *saw* a dead man walk!

In another example, prior to his crucifixion and resurrection, Jesus sat with the disciples during the Feast of Unleavened Bread (Luke 22:1).

And he took bread, gave thanks and broke it, and gave it to them, saying, "This is my body given for you; do this in remembrance of me."

In the same way, after the supper he took the cup, saying, "This cup is the new covenant in my blood, which is poured out for you."

—LUKE 22:19–20

Here Jesus has combined all three of the learning channels. The twelve *see* the bread and wine, and they become *actively involved* by eating and drinking. As they do, they *hear* the point of this lesson.

How Do You Learn?

Each of us has a learning channel, a way that we learn best. As teachers, we tend to teach the way that we prefer to learn. Since it's important to vary our teaching, it is helpful to know our own learning channel. Then we will be more inclined to incorporate the other channels into our teaching methodology.

To help you discover your learning channel, take this simple test listed on pages 61–62. First, read the question in bold. Then, of the three choices in the following row, put a check in the box that best represents you. Finally, total the checks in each column. The column with the most checks is your strongest learning channel.

Do You Learn by "Seeing," "Hearing," or "Doing"?

Read the question in bold. Of the three choices in the following row, put a check in the box that most represents you. Total the checks in each column. The column with the most checks is your strongest learning channel.

On a "free" night, would you rather:
- ❏ Read a book
- ❏ Go to the movies
- ❏ Spend time with friends having fun

For a missions trip would you rather:
- ❏ See pictures of the people and places
- ❏ Watch a movie about the people and places
- ❏ Visit the country and experience it yourself

To have fun would you:
- ❏ Visit a museum
- ❏ Watch television
- ❏ Play games

When you study the Bible do you:
- ❏ Read your notes over and over
- ❏ Repeat the information aloud
- ❏ Rewrite your notes

With a new computer do you:
- ❏ Carefully review the instructions
- ❏ Listen to the instructions
- ❏ Try it yourself— without instructions

While driving to church do you:
- ❏ Prefer quiet to enjoy the scenery
- ❏ Play your music very loudly
- ❏ Switch the channels from station to station

In Bible study do you:
- ❏ Love handouts and overheads
- ❏ Prefer to listen to the teacher
- ❏ Take lots of notes but never reread them

In your room or home do you:
- ❏ Keep it very neat all the time
- ❏ Feel that it's as clean as it needs to be
- ❏ Rearrange the furniture often

When you're excited do you:
- ❏ Write notes in your journal
- ❏ Talk with enthusiasm
- ❏ Clap your hands and jump up and down

At your desk do you:
- ❏ Decorate your workspace
- ❏ Have soft music playing
- ❏ Play games and do puzzles on a computer

To learn a new language do you:
- ☐ Like to see the words in a book
- ☐ Like to hear the words from a tape
- ☐ Like to talk with the people

In church service do you:
- ☐ Sit still for long periods of time
- ☐ Talk to your neighbor
- ☐ Become restless and have to move

To organize yourself do you:
- ☐ Write notes in your datebook
- ☐ Remember the appointment time
- ☐ Put sticky notes on the wall calendar

During your Bible quiet time do you:
- ☐ Read your Bible and pray
- ☐ Listen to gospel or praise music and pray
- ☐ Take a walk and pray

To volunteer at church do you:
- ☐ Help organize events
- ☐ Join committees and discuss plans
- ☐ Decorate, repair, or clean up

With your prayer partner do you:
- ☐ Make an appointment to meet in person
- ☐ Talk for hours on the phone
- ☐ Plan an activity together

To remember Scripture do you:
- ☐ Write the verse on cards and read it over
- ☐ Repeat the Scripture until you know it
- ☐ Develop a fun way to remember the verse

In school are you:
- ☐ The teacher's pet
- ☐ Always asking or answering questions
- ☐ First to volunteer to hand out papers

For accountability do you:
- ☐ Keep a journal or diary
- ☐ Tell your prayer partner your progress
- ☐ Attend discipleship groups

During praise and worship do you:
- ☐ Concentrate on the words
- ☐ Concentrate on the music
- ☐ Dance or move to the beat or rhythm

Are your favorite words:
- ☐ "I know ..."
- ☐ "I hear ..."
- ☐ "I can ..."

Totals:

_____ I see   _____ I hear   _____ I do

Channel Reinforcement

Using several channels in one lesson is perhaps the most effective way to teach. By addressing the learning channels of all of your students, you are insuring that they will remember the lesson. Reinforcement occurs when the same point is emphasized in several different ways.

Imagine how powerful an image the cross was for the disciples! They were eyewitnesses of the crucifixion, but then they *saw* the empty tomb. When Jesus came into their midst, they *saw* him and *talked* with him (John 20:19–31).

As teachers, we would be wise to follow in the steps of Jesus. The point of our lessons can be maximized if we utilize each channel in our teaching.

In a series I taught for women on the book of Ruth, we were examining Naomi's courage to leave dead things behind. In order to go ahead with her life, Naomi had decided to leave her dead husband, her dead sons, and her dead dreams.

Women in the class were asked to examine any area of "deadness" in their lives, anything they might be clinging to that prevented them from moving forward. They were given slips of paper on which to write the name of the person, perhaps from a relationship that had died for which they still had hopes, or a dead thing such as a habit, thought, or lifestyle that resulted in deadness.

As they were writing, I slipped into the hallway and put on a black academic robe. I reentered the sanctuary walking slowly and reading as if for a funeral procession. Behind me, one of my helpers pushed a real coffin into the room.

The women gasped! I opened the coffin—it was empty! After they recovered, they were instructed to march past the coffin and drop in their slips of paper. That night, we *saw*, we *heard*, and we *experienced* as we buried dead things. The class ended with the exhortation that no one was to be a grave robber!

One of my former students, Karen Choi, developed a Sunday school lesson for her students in Korea. Using the Ten Commandments, she designed a series to help her learners shed some social and cultural baggage.

When she taught the first commandment, "You shall have no other gods before me" (Exod. 20:3), she encouraged her students to identify the gods of other religions—Buddha, the Greek gods, the various Japanese idols, and Korean ancestors who are revered to the point of having godlike qualities. In addition, students learned that anything—television, clothes, food, drugs, and an obsession with getting good grades—can become an idol, if it takes priority over God.

For the second commandment, "You shall not make for yourself an idol in the form of anything in heaven above or on the earth beneath or in the waters below. You shall not bow down to them or worship them" (Exod. 20:4–5), Karen designed the following lesson. Before the students arrived, she set up a "Je-sah" table at the head of the classroom. Je-sah is the Korean tradition where one bows before dead ancestors to ask for blessing, protection, and long life. A framed picture of the deceased, fruit, and lit candles were on the table.

After her class entered the room and settled down, Karen said, "We are confronted sometimes at social events, such as family gatherings, with bowing to our ancestors. But it is crystal clear that we are breaking the second commandment if we take part in this seemingly innocent and traditional practice." The presence of the Je-sah in the church provided a powerful visual for her students and served as a concrete reference point for her lesson.

To capitalize on having her students' attention, Karen explained that visiting "Do-sahs" or fortune-tellers, and indulging in "Sa-ju," a common practice for brides-to-be to see how their marriage will turn out, also violate Scripture. For students who participated in these without realizing that they were disobeying God, the lesson ended with a prayer asking forgiveness.

Masterful Methods

As God, Jesus understood the people, his learners. He knew what they knew, and he knew what they needed to know. Because they were like sheep without a shepherd, he guided, directed, motivated, and sometimes even angered them. But always, he taught—masterfully, creatively, powerfully.

Once we begin to think in terms of *see, hear,* and *do,* all in the same lesson, our teaching becomes multidimensional. Learning channels plus varying the methods leads to masterful teaching. Jesus instructed us to use the treasures in our storehouses (Matt. 13:52). As with any storage place, once we begin to open the boxes, we'll find that there is so much from which to choose!

As we have already observed in Jesus' teaching, rarely did he use the same method twice. He even healed blind people differently (Mark 8:22–26; Luke 18:35–43). To help vary our methods so that our lessons are memorable, see pages 66–67 for a suggested list of activities. Can you categorize these *show*, *tell*, and *do* methods by putting a check next to the appropriate activity? Remember that the worst method to use is the one you use all the time! (See appendix B for the "Answer Key.")

Imagine! There is more than one way to teach! Once we open our storehouses, there are endless, creative possibilities. Students will be excited about coming to class because they won't know what to expect.

Some of the country's leading senior pastors even realize that the sermon or lecture is not always the most effective way for their members to learn, and they have been bold enough to try something different. Rather than the traditional sermon at special occasions such as Christmas or Easter, for example, pastors might deliver the Word in

Note: Several of these activities may fall into two or even three categories. Choose the category that is dominant.

	Show (Visual)	Tell (Auditory)	Do (Kinesthetic)
1. Conduct a demonstration	_____	_____	_____
2. Display a clip from television	_____	_____	_____
3. Do no-talk teacher*	_____	_____	_____
4. Prepare a speech or lecture	_____	_____	_____
5. Use an overhead projector	_____	_____	_____
6. Have small-group discussion	_____	_____	_____
7. Complete this story	_____	_____	_____
8. Write a skit or play	_____	_____	_____
9. Play games	_____	_____	_____
10. Take a trip	_____	_____	_____
11. Make a poster	_____	_____	_____
12. Listen to a testimony	_____	_____	_____
13. Sing a solo or group song	_____	_____	_____
14. Go for a hospital visit	_____	_____	_____
15. Listen to a song on a CD	_____	_____	_____
16. Draw or color	_____	_____	_____
17. Visualize or imagine	_____	_____	_____
18. Paraphrase a passage	_____	_____	_____
19. Read in unison	_____	_____	_____
20. Do question-and-answer	_____	_____	_____
21. Discuss in neighbor nudge	_____	_____	_____
22. Cook a meal/eat a meal	_____	_____	_____
23. Say a sentence prayer	_____	_____	_____
24. Conduct an interview	_____	_____	_____
25. Have a puppet show	_____	_____	_____
26. Keep a journal	_____	_____	_____
27. Tell an account with flannelgraph	_____	_____	_____
28. See a movie	_____	_____	_____
29. Complete a puzzle	_____	_____	_____
30. Play the Bible drill	_____	_____	_____
31. Memorize a verse	_____	_____	_____
32. Repeat the Bible account	_____	_____	_____
33. Make arts and crafts	_____	_____	_____
34. Take a test	_____	_____	_____

*In "no-talk teacher," the teacher enters the classroom but does not say anything. For example, the teacher may sit at the desk and "pretend" to be asleep, sad, or otherwise disengaged. Students react to the "silence" in the room.

cont.	Show	Tell	Do
35. Find the Scripture	_____	_____	_____
36. Write a letter	_____	_____	_____
37. Agree/disagree discussion	_____	_____	_____
38. Unscramble the verses	_____	_____	_____
39. Listen to a tape recording	_____	_____	_____
40. Take a walk	_____	_____	_____
41. Find locations on a map	_____	_____	_____
42. Unscramble the words	_____	_____	_____
43. Play instruments	_____	_____	_____
44. Answer in circle response	_____	_____	_____
45. Post on bulletin board	_____	_____	_____
46. Finger paint	_____	_____	_____
47. Do a dramatic reading	_____	_____	_____
48. Compose a poem	_____	_____	_____
49. Give a ten-minute sermon	_____	_____	_____
50. Dress up as a Bible character	_____	_____	_____
51. Paraphrase a hymn	_____	_____	_____
52. Write a commercial	_____	_____	_____
53. Do spontaneous drama	_____	_____	_____
54. Make a collage	_____	_____	_____
55. Brainstorm	_____	_____	_____
56. Write poetry/psalm	_____	_____	_____
57. Write out a Bible verse	_____	_____	_____
58. Dialogue	_____	_____	_____
59. Make a mural	_____	_____	_____
60. Do role-play	_____	_____	_____
61. Debate	_____	_____	_____
62. Make charts	_____	_____	_____
63. Write a prayer	_____	_____	_____
64. Compare songs	_____	_____	_____
65. Pantomime	_____	_____	_____
66. Record a report	_____	_____	_____
67. Write a character comparison	_____	_____	_____
68. Solve a problem	_____	_____	_____
69. Do creative writing	_____	_____	_____
70. Make a video	_____	_____	_____
71. Perform a sociodrama (social problem)	_____	_____	_____
72. Write original songs	_____	_____	_____
73. Paint	_____	_____	_____
74. Do paper cuts	_____	_____	_____
75. Make a mobile	_____	_____	_____

character dressed as Joseph, Mary, or Peter. How refreshing to hear the "sermon" from the lips of one who was actually "there." The congregation sees, hears, and experiences the Word of God in a fresh, new, and exciting way.

A Word About Small Groups

Another way to vary our teaching methodology is to utilize small groups in the classroom. Although Jesus occasionally taught individual learners such as Nicodemus (John 3:1–21) and the woman at the well (John 4:4–42), most of his teaching occurred in group settings and focused primarily on the disciples.

When we look at the gospel accounts, we see these groupings of the disciples:

1. The Three (Peter, James, and John)
2. The Twelve Disciples (and the Women)
3. The Twelve with the Thousands (the Multitudes)

Each of these groups forms one of three concentric circles around Jesus.

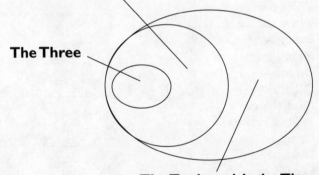

The Twelve Disciples (sometimes with the women)

The Three

The Twelve with the Thousands

Interestingly, the New Testament has no record of Jesus teaching any of the disciples alone. Because Peter was the spokesperson for the Twelve, he was usually the one asking or answering questions, offering opinions, or generally putting his foot in—well, in his case—in the water. So it may seem that Peter had a private audience, but according to the biblical account, he did not. Often when he spoke out, he did so on behalf of the other disciples, either in a small group (12) or a smaller group (3).

A major benefit of the small-group process is that students are able to learn from each other. Teaching in groups encourages the learning process in a nonthreatening way. It implies that everyone is important; everyone can contribute. Since no one person is expected to know everything, group members can explain their information to one another, which, in the process, makes them feel valued and respected.

In the educational arena, capitalizing on the group-learning process is called *cooperative learning*. Cooperative learning helps us accept each other's weaknesses and applaud each other's strengths. We learn to cooperate with one another rather than to compete individually. While some corporations stress competition, working together as a team is vital in church ministry.

Putting people in dyads (groups of two), triads (groups of three), or quads (groups of four) is very effective. Groups can find the answers, work on projects, discuss passages of Scripture, or share their own experiences. An effective method is to divide the teaching hour so that students in their groups have time to solve a problem, discuss or debate a point, search the Scriptures, or answer questions.

The youth teacher had grown increasingly frustrated with the class. The church was in transition and used a high school in South Central Los Angeles as its Sunday morning location. In a way this was a bonus, because the same students who attended the school during the week began to wander across to their campus and visit this new "church" on Sunday mornings. What great evangelism! But classes had become quite large, and teaching soon became a fruitless exercise.

The teacher, used to smaller classes and one-on-one discussion, struggled to find a way of relating. Finally, out of desperation, a decision was made. Rather than lecture, why not give the class a project?

When students arrived the next Sunday, a handout sheet and pencils were waiting for them on their desks. Working together in small groups, their activity was to fill in the blanks. Together, students had to read the Bible passage and find the correct answers themselves.

It seemed like a different class. Students talked and worked together, obviously engaged with the assignment. That morning, learning occurred.

In the monthly teachers' meeting, this seasoned veteran remarked that we often miss the obvious. Because of their Monday to Friday learning environment, students are familiar with such assignments. Just give them paper and a pencil! It's how they learn all during the week. But suddenly on Sunday mornings we expect them to sit still and listen to a lecture. We become frustrated with our students' inattentiveness. Rather than endeavoring to be effective teachers, we become disgruntled baby-sitters.

Remember, if people can communicate, they like working in small groups! It's an effective method for first graders all the way to adults. Notice, too, how methods vary depending on the size of the group. Jesus did not explain his parables to the multitudes, for instance. He explained the meaning of the parables to the disciples once they were apart from the crowds (Matt. 13:36). And the lessons for his inner circle, the Three, differed from the way that Jesus taught the larger group of disciples. Likewise, the way we use cooperative learning must be adjusted to the size of our class.

Do You Remember?

In this chapter, we compared learning channels as a way to vary methods for showing, telling, and doing. Below is a summary of the major points to remember.

- *We Learn Differently.* We must vary our teaching methods to meet the needs of our audience.
- *Jesus Taught Through "Seeing."* Handouts, pictures, use of overheads, multimedia, movie clips, television, and computers are excellent tools for students who learn through the visual channel.
- *Jesus Taught Through "Hearing."* Stories, lecture, question-and-answer, and audio tapes are a few examples of teaching students who learn through the auditory channel.
- *Jesus Taught Through "Doing."* Students who learn through the kinesthetic channel prefer to be physically involved in the lesson.
- *Combining Channels.* Address several channels to reinforce the lesson.

- *Masterful Methods.* Use *show, tell,* and *do* methods when we teach.
- *Small Groups.* Utilize small-group settings by placing students in clusters of three or four so that they can discuss topics with one another at some point during the teaching hour.

The Next Step

We have acquired much new information, and now we're ready for the next step. As we continue to evaluate how Jesus taught, we will now shift our attention to another important aspect of the Master Teacher.

Jesus understood how his learners *felt.* Because he cared about them emotionally, he treated his learners with respect, rewarded them to show his approval, and related what they already knew to what they were about to learn.

In other words, Jesus was in touch with his learners' world. We can do the same. It begins by stepping into our students' shoes . . . or skates!

Chapter 5

In the Learner's Skates
Helping Students Remember

Objective

By the end of this chapter, you will evaluate how the learner learns by considering the benefits of respecting learners, rewarding learners, relating new ideas to what learners already know, and repeating information.

In this microwaving, e-mailing, Internet world, people are moving fast! There's hardly time to really get to know them ... there's so much work to do. But as teachers, knowing our students *is* our work. Remember the saying that in order to understand people, we must "walk a mile in their shoes"? For our learning context, we will know our students better if we *skate* in their *skates*.

Characteristics and Needs

The skate diagram represents the teaching-learning world of our students neatly wrapped up in one little boot. The first part of the blade is the learners' *characteristics*. Defined primarily by age and secondarily by culture, characteristics give us helpful information about the learners.

For instance, students may be nursery or preschool age, walking or crawling. Or, students may be in elementary school and capable of reading or counting. In the case of teenagers, learners may be able to think hypothetically and comprehend abstract concepts. These are examples of characteristics, and they are dependent on the age of the student. We will look at age characteristics in more detail in Part 2.

The next part of the blade represents the *needs* of the learner. Needs vary from culture to culture, neighborhood to neighborhood, and individual to individual. They are determined by factors such as economic status, family composition, and education. Cultural needs are important considerations in the teaching-learning process.

To meet the needs of our learners, our lessons must be culturally appropriate. When we appreciate the ethnic nuances in our audience, we are careful to lace our lessons with examples that reference the lives of the people to whom we minister. Tailoring our teaching to fit the specific needs of our learners demands cultural sensitivity and spiritual discernment.

We must also be gender sensitive. Men and women have different needs, and our teaching must consider their issues as well. As teachers, we should be aware of our students' perspectives when we step into their learning environment.

The ankle of the skate that supports the learning process represents the learning channel—visual, auditory, or kinesthetic—which we discussed in the previous chapter. The bootlaces are the teaching methods we use to target each channel. Within each lesson, activities should vary, assuring us that we are reaching all of the students in our classroom.

In the Skate of the Learner

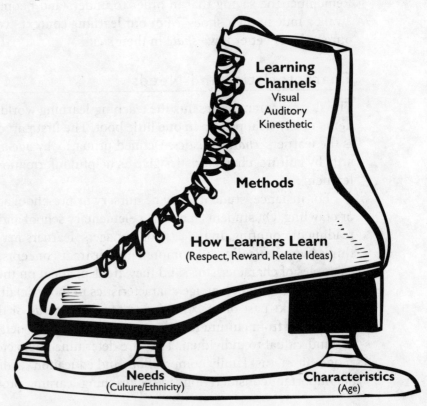

Learning Channels
Visual
Auditory
Kinesthetic

Methods

How Learners Learn
(Respect, Reward, Relate Ideas)

Needs
(Culture/Ethnicity)

Characteristics
(Age)

Respect, Reward, Relate, Repeat

The foot of the skate is the foundational support that represents how learners learn, which we are now ready to study. Treating students with *respect* shows that we value them as people. *Rewarding* students for correct answers encourages participation. *Relating* new ideas to familiar ones helps students grasp new concepts. *Repeating* information serves as reinforcement to help learners remember.

Again, Jesus, the Master Teacher, is remarkable! Nearly two thousand years ago, he gave us teaching examples to help us design our lessons today. Let's take a look at each aspect.

Jesus Respects the Learner

With individual after individual, Jesus showed his respect, care, and concern for the learner. He paid particular attention to those who, because of their gender, social status, or infirmity, were considered outcasts of society.

In the economy of the Jewish culture, women were of inferior status. In fact, rabbis used to thank God that they were not created a Gentile, a slave, or a female! Imagine, then, the displeasure of these self-righteous men as Jesus, through his words and actions, affirmed women. Throughout the course of his ministry, Jesus included, validated, healed, and forgave women, demonstrating his deep respect for them.

The account of the crippled woman is only one of many examples. There she was in the synagogue, bent over from a spirit that had prevented her from standing up straight for 18 years. Jesus saw her and called her forward. "Woman, you are set free from your infirmity" (Luke 13:12). The synagogue ruler became indignant that Jesus dared to heal on the Sabbath. Jesus responded with this sharp rebuke.

> "You hypocrites! Doesn't each of you on the Sabbath untie his ox or donkey from the stall and lead it out to give it water? Then should not this woman, a daughter of Abraham, whom Satan has kept bound for eighteen long years, be set free on the Sabbath day from what bound her?"
>
> —LUKE 13:15–16

Other women validated by Jesus were Mary Magdalene (Luke 8:2), the woman who anointed Jesus' feet (Luke 7:36–50), Mary of Bethany (Matt. 26:6–13; Luke 10:42), and the woman healed of the issue of blood (Matt. 9:20), just to name a few. Women were even included in his ministry, traveling with Jesus and the disciples (Luke 8:1–3).

Jesus also paid attention to societal outcasts like the lame (John 5:1–18), the blind (John 9), lepers (Matt. 8:2–4; Luke 17:11–19), and those who were demon possessed (Matt. 8:28–34; Mark 1:23–28). He was never too busy to stop, listen, and minister.

As teachers in the local church, it's difficult to challenge, exhort, and encourage students we don't really respect. Speaking in condescending tones, "fussing" at students continually, making fun of them under the guise of "just kidding," and calling them names are examples of negative behaviors that result from a lack of respect.

Respecting students means that we have compassion about their circumstances, appreciate their experiences, and value their comments and opinions. We especially need to respect those students who sit in our classrooms and who are quiet and less flamboyant than are other students. We never know whom God is going to use!

When I taught the junior high class, certain students always demanded my attention by asking irrelevant questions or by constantly offering their opinions at inappropriate times. Thinking these to be the ones most interested in biblical matters, I tended to pour myself into them, focusing on their needs and problems to the neglect of the more silent students.

Off to the side of the classroom sat three students who were always in attendance. These young ladies never caused a problem, and they never drew attention to themselves. They were polite, quiet, and attentive. I appreciated them because they were model students.

Still, I found myself laboring more intently with the other youth. Knowing some of their struggles at home, I tended to take them under my wing, going the extra mile to make certain they attended retreats and church events. I just knew that this expense of labor would produce fruit. How disappointed I was to see one of these students fall away from the Lord to live a life of rebellion and disobedience—everything I had tried so hard to prevent!

Praise God for bringing the challenges of ministry into perspective. Earlier this year, a young woman from the quiet group, now all grown up and a college graduate, approached me with a request. Khala Taylor had decided to attend seminary, and she asked me to write her pastoral reference. She told me that I probably did not realize the seeds I had planted in her life, and that she was encouraged by my example to pursue ministry. And what is her course of study? Christian education!

God knows whom he will use, and we don't. It's not always the most talkative student. That's why everyone must be treated with respect. As teachers, we tend to judge from outer appearances, students' performances, and a host of other superficial criteria. But God knows the heart (1 Sam. 16:7).

Respect and value for the learner are also wrapped up in the way we approach the class setting. Respecting students means that we realize that they have varying degrees of strengths and weaknesses, and we recognize and applaud everyone for what he or she is able to contribute to the teaching-learning process.

Jesus Rewards the Learner

When students answered questions correctly, Jesus rewarded them. Remember Simon Peter at Caesarea Philippi? When Jesus asked, "'Who do you say I am?' Simon Peter answered, 'You are the Christ, the Son of the living God'" (Matt. 16:15–16). Jesus rewarded Peter with this blessing.

> "Blessed are you, Simon son of Jonah, for this was not revealed to you by man, but by my Father in heaven. And I tell you that you are Peter, and on this rock I will build my church, and the gates of Hades will not overcome it."
>
> —MATTHEW 16:17–18

Of course, it was only a few verses later that Jesus disciplined Peter. Rewards and discipline work hand in hand because offering rewards makes discipline more effective. Imagine Peter's initial self-pleasure at receiving verbal praise from Jesus. Then imagine how humbled he must have felt when he responded incorrectly so soon afterward and was sharply corrected (Matt. 16:23). (We will discuss more ways to discipline later in this book.)

Rewarding students encourages them to participate. It is vital to acknowledge answers, even if they are not stated exactly as we might expect. Repeating students' answers, nodding approval, and thanking students for their suggestions are ways to reward the learner.

Rewards also come in the form of gifts or tokens. Children love to earn bookmarks or any small prize such as pencils or stars next to their names on a chart. Nursery children love stickers on their hands for good behavior.

Adults, too, love rewards. In an adult Bible study, I handed out "Early Riser" buttons with Proverbs 8:17 printed on them: "I love those who love me, and those who seek me find me." The goal was to encourage class members to awaken early in the morning and spend time with the Lord reading and praying. They had to be consistent for at least one entire week in order to receive a button. They became so motivated that we soon ran out of buttons!

Rewards work. Aren't we are all eager to receive ours?

"Well done, good and faithful servant! You have been faithful with a few things; I will put you in charge of many things. Come and share your master's happiness!"

—MATTHEW 25:21

A wonderful time to give rewards is during Vacation Bible School. Each night children and parents alike can earn "VBS Bucks" if they fulfill the requirement for the day. By the end of the week these "bucks" are redeemable, and items can be purchased from the VBS Reward Store. Here is an example of how bucks may be awarded:

HOW TO EARN "VBS BUCKS"

Monday	Bring Your Bible
Tuesday	Know Your Scripture
Wednesday	Bring a Friend
Thursday	Wear a Gospel T-shirt
Friday	Perfect VBS Attendance

Remember, rewards are *excellent* motivators.

Vacation Bible School Bucks

Jesus Relates New Ideas

To help students learn new concepts, Jesus often used questions as a bridge to relate new ideas to what learners already knew. Imagine, God Incarnate asking questions! Obviously, he didn't ask questions because he needed to know the answers. For Jesus, questions were a powerful teaching tool designed, not as a test of the students' knowledge, but as a way to stimulate the students' thinking. His questions scratched beneath the surface, sometimes revealing an impure motive or hidden agenda.

When the Pharisees questioned Jesus about divorce to test him, for example, he answered their question with a question: "Haven't you read . . . ?" (Matt. 19:4). He then clarified the divorce issue and silenced his accusers.

When the rich young ruler approached Jesus with his question, Jesus answered with a question that pointed to his deity. The young man, intent on justifying himself as perfect before God, continued to press the Teacher. By the end of this short lesson, however, the rich ruler realized that he was spiritually bankrupt.

> Now a man came up to Jesus and asked, "Teacher, what good thing must I do to get eternal life?"
>
> "Why do you ask me about what is good?" Jesus replied. "There is only One who is good. If you want to enter life, obey the commandments."
>
> "Which ones?" the man inquired.
>
> Jesus replied, "'Do not murder, do not commit adultery, do not steal, do not give false testimony, honor your father and mother,' and 'love your neighbor as yourself.'"
>
> "All these I have kept," the young man said. "What do I still lack?"
>
> Jesus answered, "If you want to be perfect, go, sell your possessions and give to the poor, and you will have treasure in heaven. Then come, follow me."
>
> When the young man heard this, he went away sad, because he had great wealth.
>
> —MATTHEW 19:16–22

In this exchange, Jesus shifted the focus from the outward adherence of the Law to the inner disposition of this man's heart—boastful, self-justifying pride. The ruler left realizing that contrary to his own self-evaluation, he was far from perfect in the sight of God. Concerned with *doing* good, Jesus instead stressed *being* good, which is impossible apart from God.

In another Q & A session, Jesus was leaving Jericho with the multitude following when two blind men at the gate asked him to be merciful to them. Jesus stopped, and then proceeded to ask them what seemed to be such an obvious question:

> "What do you want me to do for you?" he asked.
> "Lord," they answered, "we want our sight."
> Jesus had compassion on them and touched their eyes. Immediately they received their sight and followed him.
> —MATTHEW 20:32–34

Why would Jesus ask the obvious? Here they were, blind men, sitting by the roadside, probably begging, and Jesus asks what they want from him. Their answer to his question—a request to restore their sight—results in their healing.

Just a few verses earlier, a mother had approached Jesus with an unwise request. With her two sons by her side, she asked that one be allowed to sit at the right hand of Jesus, the other at his left.

> Then the mother of Zebedee's sons came to Jesus with her sons and, kneeling down, asked a favor of him.
> "What is it you want?" he asked.
> She said, "Grant that one of these two sons of mine may sit at your right and the other at your left in your kingdom."
> "You don't know what you are asking," Jesus said to them. "Can you drink the cup I am going to drink?"
> "We can," they answered.
> Jesus said to them, "You will indeed drink from my cup, but to sit at my right or left is not for me to grant. These places belong to those for whom they have been prepared by my Father."
> —MATTHEW 20:20–23

What an unwise request! These two sons may have their eyesight, but seeing, they didn't perceive. Immediately afterward, Jesus encountered two men who were physically blind. He asked them their request, and rather than asking foolishly, they asked for the help they needed. Though blind, they "saw" and understood.

Many more examples of how Jesus effectively asked—and answered—questions are tucked within the Gospels. As a teaching method, asking the right question is a powerful tool. Questions can help students discover truth by taking them from where they are to where they need to be. Framing questions properly is like climbing up the steps of a ladder.

Step 1

At the bottom of the ladder are questions that ask what students know or understand. These *knowledge* questions are basic, and students' answers are often derived from memory. Who, what, where, when, and how are all knowledge questions. This level of questioning is appropriate for the early stages of learning new information or for teaching children. Examples include:

- What happened at Pentecost?
- Who is Mary?
- How many books are there in the Bible?

Step 2

At the next step up the ladder, questions test the students' *comprehension*. These ask students to restate what was read, studied, or learned, to paraphrase or put the information into their own words, or to compare, contrast, or explain the main idea. To answer these questions, students must comprehend what they have learned. Examples:

- Restate the biblical account of the birth of Jesus in your own words.
- Explain what Jesus meant in the parable of the soils.
- Compare and contrast the priest and the Samaritan in the parable of the Good Samaritan by acting out this scenario in a modern-day setting.

Step 3

The next rung on the ladder pertains to questions on *application*. These ask students to make a selection or give one right answer. They may choose from several options, write an example, solve a problem, apply, or organize information. In this application step, there is only one correct answer. Examples are:

- How does Jesus want us to remember his death and resurrection? By being baptized, by taking Communion, or by going to church?
- Categorize the books of the Old Testament.
- List the main events preceding the Crucifixion.

Step 4

A higher level of questions on the *analysis* step asks students to answer the question "Why?" Students must distinguish or analyze, so they must have the ability to think hypothetically. Depending on the lesson, some children in preschool through fifth grade may be able to answer "Why?" but generally, students in this age group are not yet able to think in the abstract. Analysis questions are more effectively used with students who are mature. These questions ask students to identify reasons, look at causes, draw conclusions, find supporting evidence, analyze, and find motives. Examples are:

- Analyze the parable of the five wise virgins and the five foolish virgins.
- Why did Joseph decide to run from Potiphar's wife? According to the biblical account, what was his primary motive?
- Analyze the prayer that Jesus taught his disciples. What should every prayer contain?

Step 5

Further up this question ladder, we reach the *synthesis* step. Here students may be asked to plan, design, develop, draw, or find a solution. Students must be able to solve problems or produce something original based on what they have learned. There may be many ways to answer a synthesis question. Examples are:

- Plan your own lesson on the book of Jonah.
- Design a mission statement for your small-group project.
- Outline the book of Ruth.

Step 6

At the highest level, the top step of the ladder, is *evaluation*. Here students must make a decision. They are asked to judge, decide which is better, give their opinions, or agree that a certain course of action is preferred. Students make decisions based on their evaluation of the options. Examples are:

- Is it better to accept or to reject Jesus Christ as your Savior?
- From the account of Shadrach, Meshach, and Abednego in Daniel 3, what is one choice you can make to handle peer pressure at school?
- Based on 1 John 3:9, how would you evaluate a person who habitually, continually, deliberately practices sin?

In the educational arena, these six levels of questioning are referred to as "Bloom's Taxonomy." These steps are designed to assist students in discovering information by answering questions and finding solutions. We will discuss later how to plan a lesson using these steps.

Bloom's Taxonomy

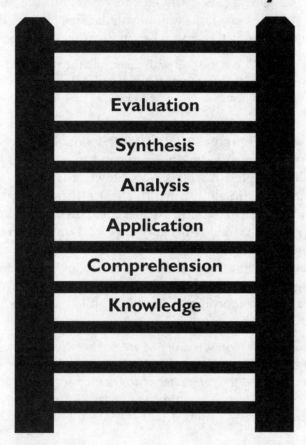

Evaluation

Synthesis

Analysis

Application

Comprehension

Knowledge

As stated previously, asking the right questions allows students to discover information on their own. When they dig into the Scriptures themselves, truths uncovered will not be buried in forgetfulness. Spoon-feeding students creates dependency on the teacher. Rather than simply preparing and serving their food for them, why not let them make their own meals?

Disequilibrium and Discovery Learning

Jesus knew that students learn when they have to discover information on their own. They may experience *disequilibrium*—an uncomfortable feeling that results because the perception of reality has been disrupted—but they will learn! Allowing students to dig for the information themselves is called *discovery learning*.

When Jesus walked on water, he used discovery learning. Remember the scene? During the early morning hours in the middle of a storm, the disciples saw Jesus walking on the lake towards their boat. They were so frightened because they thought they had seen a ghost!

> Then he climbed into the boat with them, and the wind died down. They were completely amazed, for they had not understood about the loaves; their hearts were hardened.
>
> —MARK 6:51–52

What was the purpose of this lesson? Through the supernatural healings, provision of food, and command over nature, Jesus was teaching the disciples that he is God. Slowly, they began to understand. When they finally learned this truth, these men turned the world upside down (Acts 17:6)! No one could dissuade them! No one could stop them! Wouldn't it be wonderful if our students felt the same way too?

Discovery learning works today as the following example illustrates. Imagine the disequilibrium experienced by these learners when their entire Sunday morning was suddenly filled with free time!

The congregation was stunned when, after spirited praise and worship, Steve West, pastor of A.W.A.N.A. Bible Fellowship in Los Angeles, canceled the remainder of the church service.

"There will not be any preaching today. Go and do what you have been learning," he instructed. "Maybe we'll have church next Sunday."

With that announcement, church was dismissed. For African-Americans accustomed to lengthy morning services, this was traumatic.

The pastor explained. For several weeks, he had been teaching a series on evangelism. His members were learning how to share their faith with unbelievers, how to witness, how to lead people to Christ. Sunday after Sunday they came to church, took notes, and went home. Finally, this particular Sunday, when the pastor looked out into the congregation and did not see even one new face, he realized that people were not practicing what they had been learning.

"Why continue with more information until they do what they already know?" he said. The next Sunday, several new faces dotted the congregation.

Discovery learning demands willingness on the part of the teacher to take risks. Knowing the students well is key. Playing what's commonly known as "devil's advocate" and using role playing are additional discovery learning methods.

The high school class had just learned how to share their faith based on the "Four Spiritual Laws." They had learned many Scriptures about leading a friend to Christ and had come to class prepared for a "test."

Into the room wandered a man who was apparently lost. He was dressed like a Muslim, and he carried a Koran. He introduced himself as Makungu Akinyela and asked if he could sit in the class for a while. The students graciously said yes.

As they began their review, this visitor asked questions and gently challenged their statements based, of course, on the writings in the Koran. The students scrambled to find the right verses in their Bibles in defense of the Gospel. Some were frustrated because they could not locate quickly enough the answers they knew were in the Bible—information that they had studied.

Finally, toward the end of the class, this "visitor" introduced himself and acknowledged that he was not actually a Muslim. In fact, he was a good friend of their teacher. He was asked to play "devil's advocate" to test what the students had learned. His final advice to the class was this: When trying to share your faith, share your personal testimony. People can argue and debate all day long, but what they cannot challenge is the personal change that Jesus Christ has made in an individual's life.

Although these young men and women couldn't believe that they fell so completely for this "visitor," they all agreed that this was a lesson they would never forget. Through disequilibrium and discovery learning, they learned the key to sharing their faith—the point of the entire series of lessons.

Such methods are creative and powerful, similar to Jesus allowing Peter to sink when he attempted to walk on the water (Matt. 14:25–33). Obviously, Jesus was not going to let Peter drown, but letting him get wet helped Peter to evaluate his faith. Such teaching techniques, while neither possible nor advisable to use too frequently, are valuable tools when the time is right.

Framing Our Lesson

Jesus also knew that the disciples learned effectively if they had a *frame* upon which to hang their lessons. For example, by giving them the "big picture" and summarizing in advance what to expect before his suffering and crucifixion, the disciples were given a frame upon which to analyze these difficult events when they actually occurred (John 12:23).

At the beginning of our lessons, we can give our students the big picture by framing our lessons with an overview. Example: "Today we will begin our study in chapter one of the book of John. We will examine Jesus—his deity and his eternality."

Or if we are studying books of the Bible such as Acts, we can frame our lessons by giving students a big picture of how the book is divided. With this overview, the details in the chapters make more sense. For example, "Here is the key to the entire book of Acts, which we will begin studying today."

> "But you will receive power when the Holy Spirit comes on you; and you will be my witnesses in Jerusalem, and in all Judea and Samaria, and to the ends of the earth."
>
> —Acts 1:8

The frame may also include a written outline of the book:

Acts 1–7	Jerusalem
Acts 8–12	Judea and Samaria
Acts 13–28	The ends of the earth

The big picture will be even clearer if students are given a drawing, a visual that they can remember:

Acts Advanced Organizer

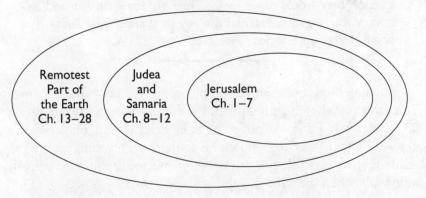

Remotest Part of the Earth Ch. 13–28

Judea and Samaria Ch. 8–12

Jerusalem Ch. 1–7

Metaphors or word pictures are excellent ways to relate new ideas or concepts to what students have already learned. Again, Jesus is our model. He understood that new information is easier to grasp when it is experienced in the familiar.

Let's refer back to the example we just used in explaining the big picture where Jesus alerted his disciples in advance of his impending crucifixion. To draw a picture of his death's reproductive nature—the many souls that would result from his sacrifice—Jesus used the metaphor of a "kernel of wheat" that produces many seeds once it falls to the ground and dies (John 12:24). Only later would the disciples fully grasp the meaning of these words. But at least they had a picture in their minds, an example they would remember.

On another occasion Jesus used word pictures to teach important truths to Peter and his brother Andrew, who were fishermen. "Come, follow me," Jesus said, "and I will make you fishers of men" (Matt. 4:19). By using a metaphor and comparing fishing with the ministry of fishing for people, Jesus helped these learners understand their purpose in following him. Throughout his ministry, Jesus used metaphors to help his learners grasp his deity. The chart below highlights some of them.

Jesus Used Metaphors to Teach About His Deity

Jesus, the Living Word, became flesh.

Jesus, the Living Water, turned water into wine.

Jesus, the Light of the World, opened the eyes of the blind.

Jesus, the Bread of Life, fed the multitudes.

Jesus, the Great Physician, healed the sick.

Jesus, the Good Shepherd, gave his life for the sheep.

Jesus, the Resurrection and the Life, raised the dead.

Metaphors, painting word pictures, and speaking within the context of the learner's everyday life are ways to connect the new with the familiar.

To explain to an adult Bible class that "sin" means to "miss the mark," I purchased a game to help with the illustration. It was designed like a dart board with a bulls-eye in the center. Plastic balls, approximately the size of golf balls, were covered in Velcro so they would stick to the board when thrown.

Before class began, I hung the board on the wall. When it came time for the illustration, I asked volunteers to stand and try to hit the bulls-eye. Everyone aimed for the center, but no one landed perfectly. With every miss, regardless of how far away or how close the ball landed to the center, I had the entire class shout, "Sin!" These adults had fun trying to hit center. The men, with their athletic sense of competition, especially enjoyed the exercise.

Afterwards I explained, "Sin means to miss the mark. We all do our best to be good, but no matter how hard we try, 'all have sinned and fall short of the glory of God' (Rom. 3:23). It doesn't matter how good we are, just as it didn't matter how close to the center the ball landed. If it doesn't land right in the center, it's sin. Even if we miss the board completely, it's still sin. Landing almost at the center or landing a foot from the center is the same—sin. That's why we need a Savior."

Think of the metaphors used so frequently in the Christian faith to help us understand important concepts. There's the faith walk where we are led blindfolded around the room to experience the truth that "We walk by faith, not by sight" (2 Cor. 5:7 KJV).

And then there's the butterfly. The ugly caterpillar, which represents our old sin nature, is transformed into one of God's most beautiful creatures. What better picture of the remarkable transformation that occurs in the life of the believer than the caterpillar that becomes a butterfly (Rom. 12:1–2)!

Because these concepts—faith and transformation—are related to ideas already present in our minds, we are able to comprehend profound biblical truths. Relating new concepts to ideas that students already know is essential.

Old Worms have Passed Away Look! Everyone's a Butterfly!

*Therefore, if anyone is in Christ,
he is a new creation;
the old has gone, the new has come.
(2 Cor. 5:17)*

Repeat to Remember

Repetition is the mother of teaching. Repetition helps students remember. Jesus repeated types of miracles, his warnings to the Pharisees and Sadducees, and his teachings on the kingdom. Why not skim through the Scriptures and find your own examples of other themes that Jesus repeated?

In addition to repetition, we can help students remember information by using mnemonic devices, or memory techniques, such as alliteration. Alliteration uses words that begin with the same first letter of the alphabet. The main points in this chapter have been arranged according to this principle—**R**espect students; **R**eward students; **R**elate new ideas; **R**epeat information.

Acrostics are another example of mnemonic techniques that help students remember. In the introduction, we used this acrostic to summarize the mission of Christian education: TEACH.

T rain teachers
E quip parents
A ssess ministries
C hallenge excellence
H olistically meet needs

Depending on the age group, rhymes and "raps" are also excellent mnemonic techniques that help students remember biblical information. For example, Don Stabler, a children's church volunteer teacher, wrote the following "rap song" to help students remember their lesson about Samuel (1 Sam. 1–3). The entire class learned this rap and thrilled the church congregation by reciting it during the Sunday morning service.

Is God Calling You?

Listen, little children, and you shall hear
The story of Samuel so young, so dear
You think you're small, and you don't know better
But Jesus is the answer in any kind of weather

(Chorus)
Yo, yo, is God calling you?
Yo, yo, will you know what to do?
Yo, yo, will you hear God's voice?
Yo, yo, will you make the right choice?

Samuel, a young boy, called by name
Living for God his life proclaimed
God called Samuel to do his will
To carry his word to all Israel

(Chorus)

You think you're too young to be understood
But you're never alone, so always do good
Your best friend is Jesus; yes, he's the Man
So live by God's law, be the best kid you can

(Chorus)

Be like Samuel—dedicated to God
Say, "Lord, here I am, I'm ready to start"
The Lord was with Samuel as he grew
He did it for him; he'll do it for you

(Chorus)

—Don Stabler

Emphasizing the first few words, using creative humor, and reviewing what you've covered periodically as you teach and at the end of your lesson are additional ways to help students remember. Have students visualize themselves involved in the action. Help students draw mental pictures. To memorize a verse, ask them to repeat it out loud. Remember, creative teachers make certain that they *teach*. Let's use our acrostic again, this time to demonstrate how to help our students remember.

T ell it in different ways
E xplain with metaphors and word pictures
A ct it out
C reate colorful charts and visuals
H ighlight points and emphasize key words

Do You Remember?

In this chapter, we followed the model of Jesus and focused on how the learner learns. Here is a summary of major points to remember.

- *Respect the Learner.* Value your students, and treat them with special care . . . especially the quiet ones!
- *Reward the Learner.* Repeat their answers for the entire class to hear. Give tokens to reward students and to encourage them to participate.
- *Relate New Ideas.* Relate new ideas to what learners already know. Ask questions to stimulate their thinking (use the ladder!). Encourage students to discover information on their own (even if it causes *disequilibrium!*). At the beginning of class, *frame* the lesson by presenting the "big picture." Use metaphors as a way to connect new information to information students already know.
- *Repeat the Information.* Use mnemonic or memory techniques such as alliteration, acrostics, and rhymes to help learners remember. Summarize and repeat information.

Leader's Tip

In your teacher training seminars, list and discuss the ways that Jesus helped learners to learn. Give examples and Scripture references.

Respect Learners
Reward Learners
Relate New Ideas
Repeat Information

Now, divide students into small groups so that they can do some discovery work on their own. The task? Find examples where Jesus *repeated* information in the Gospels.

Putting It All Together

Each aspect of the teaching-learning process fits together like pieces of a puzzle. Now it's time to put it all together! In Part 2 of this book, we will discuss lesson planning and how to teach according to the student's age level—children, youth, and adults.

Ready? Set? *Go!*

Leader's Tip

Retype the memory tasks below onto brightly colored paper. Cut the page into strips where indicated; divide the class into quads; give each group one strip. (Two groups may have the same task, depending on the size of your class.) Ask:

How would we help students remember . . .

Allow 10 minutes for group discussion. Each group should report back to the entire class at large.

1. The names of the twelve disciples to a sixth grade class?
----
2. The chronological order of events of Passion Week (the week prior to Easter Sunday) to a junior high group?
----
3. The books of the New Testament to a third grade class?
----
4. The seven days of Creation to a group of college freshmen?
----
5. The fruit of the Spirit to a single adult Bible study class (ages 25–35)?

Part Two
Practice for Ministry

Chapter 6

Pray ... Plan ... Prepare
Prayer, Lesson Preparation, and Curriculum Development

Objective

By the end of this chapter, you will decide to teach creatively by evaluating the importance of prayer, planning, and preparation in designing lessons.

reative teaching does not happen by accident. It results from ample time set aside to pray, plan, and prepare. When these are our priorities, the Holy Spirit breathes life into our lessons . . . and into our learners.

The Prayer Channel

Learning channels are the means by which learners receive information. Prayer is the channel through which we receive power, strength, and guidance from God. As we plan our lessons, it is encouraging to remember that although God completed the process of revelation in his written Word and his living Son, he continues to personally guide women and men today. As we request divine guidance and direction, God provides us with the creativity and ability to develop lessons that build his truth into the lives of his followers.

What should we teach? How should we teach it? How will we get our students' attention? How will we transition from one point to the next? What illustrations work best? How will we close our lessons? How will we draw students back for the next class? Since this is the Lord's work, we must ask him for help and assistance.

Praying regularly with someone who shares your passion for ministry will provide a fortress of encouragement and support. Once in the auditorium or classroom, you have confidence in knowing that your prayer partner has whispered your name into the Father's ear. Such prayer ushers the Holy Spirit's power into your body, mind, and spirit to strengthen, shield, and empower you. Setting aside regular times to pray for your ministry creates the awareness that it is God's work; we teach in concert with his will.

So the first step in teaching is to fall on our knees. Because nothing is so powerful as the liberating weapon of God's truth, demonic forces mobilize when we teach. The enemy does not want truth to penetrate the minds and hearts of our students since he knows what knowing the truth will do.

> If you hold to my teaching, you are really my disciples. Then you will know the truth, and the truth will set you free.
>
> —John 8:31–32

Through prayer, we tear down the strongholds that would imprison the thought processes of our learners.

> For though we live in the world, we do not wage war as the world does. The weapons we fight with are not the weapons of the world. On the contrary, they have divine power to demolish strongholds. We demolish arguments and every pretension that sets itself up against the knowledge of God, and we take captive every thought to make it obedient to Christ.
>
> —2 Corinthians 10:3–5

To underestimate the seriousness of our mission to teach is to walk into the front lines of battle unarmed. To minimize the power that resides in the teaching ministry is to be as careless as flaunting jewels in a junkyard.

Remember what happens when God's truth enters the personality? Transformation occurs! Learners become more like Christ. Oh, the power of teaching. We must pray!

———

I had become desperate. The high school class was more out of control than usual. The dynamics of the group literally made teaching next to impossible.

One morning on my way to prepare for class, I passed the counseling room. I stopped to observe when I noticed that the person who gave leadership to that ministry was walking around the room praying. As she prayed, she touched the chairs and walls of the room. *How nice,* I thought as I continued to my classroom.

Once inside, I was filled with dread of what the morning held in store. True, these students weren't "bad." After all, most of them came to class on their own. No parent ushered them into the class-room. And for this, I was very grateful. But they were undisciplined. They couldn't listen or work together without throwing paper and being silly. Getting them to focus was fruitless.

Yet, these were the very ones who needed the reality of God's Word exercised in their lives. Crushed with society's view of who they were as African-Americans, they needed to see themselves from God's point of view. His truth needed to penetrate their minds. But most of the time, the class disintegrated into chaos.

I thought back to the scene I had just witnessed. Now, rather than thinking it was "nice," I wondered if prayer would really work in this situation. I decided to swap my usual short prayer to inter-cede just as I had witnessed in the counseling room. Hesitant at first, I, too, walked around my classroom.

Immediately, the Holy Spirit brought to mind images that described the actions and attitudes of my students—silliness, con-fusion, disruption, disobedience, distraction. I spoke this out loud and prayed that the Father would expel evil influences from the environment. I asked him to release his power, his peace, his pres-ence, and his control in the students in my class.

That morning, a miracle occurred. I witnessed the unbelievable power of prayer. I say unbelievable, because even while the class was in progress, I stood amazed! Students walked into the room calmly, sat down, and for the first time were teachable. They remained this way for the *entire* class.

I was startled at the difference. Never again did I underestimate the power of prayer. And never again did I minimize how serious the devil is about keeping us from effectively teaching God's truth, the Bible, to God's people.

Finally, be strong in the Lord and in his mighty power. Put on the full armor of God so that you can take your stand against the devil's schemes. For our struggle is not against flesh and blood, but against the rulers, against the authorities, against the powers of this dark world and against the spiritual forces of evil in the heavenly realms.

—EPHESIANS 6:10–12

As we plan and as we prepare, we must pray. God will fight in the spirit realm to dispel the evil forces seeking to distract our students. This is his will. During class, if we discern opposition, we may need to stop and pray. The prayer does not have to be long or loud. Just quietly speak words of peace and release, remembering that "the one who is in you is greater than the one who is in the world" (1 John 4:4).

As we pray in front of our students, whether for class control, for wisdom, or for their needs, we model to them that our reliance is on God. We take the backseat and acknowledge that God is in the driver's seat. Then when they find themselves in trouble, our students will remember to pray, too.

Heung was raised in Korea. His mother was a devout Buddhist. His father was also a Buddhist, but he was not as strong a believer as was his wife. One day, Heung's friend invited him to attend church, and without even thinking about it, he went. That day he accepted Jesus Christ as his Savior. When he arrived home and told his mother about his decision, she was extremely upset.

Even though Heung knew that attending church was against her wishes, he would sneak out of the house to attend with his friend. During this time Heung confided in his youth pastor who encouraged him to pray.

It didn't take long for his mother to change her mind. In fact, much to Heung's surprise, she announced that she would like to visit the church. Today both parents are saved. And Heung, who learned the power of prayer early in his Christian life, is now a pastor.

Here is one final example that demonstrates the power of prayer.

It was my day to volunteer in the nursery. By the third service, we were exhausted, but the children kept arriving. The parents' silent but desperate plea to take "just one more child" made it difficult to refuse anyone, but we were quickly reaching our maximum.

They must have been the last two children we accepted. Their father dropped them off, a two-year-old brother and his three-year-old sister. I remembered the family from their visit to the church office for assistance from our pastor of community services. These children had been removed from their mother, a drug addict, and placed with their father. Both had been born with cocaine in their systems.

After five minutes, our nursery was in a state of chaos! This little girl, dressed daintily in her floral-print dress, seemed to have invisible roller skates attached to the bottom of her shoes. She was pulling books off the shelves, taking toys from the other children, trying to remove the protective plastic covering on the electrical sockets, pulling barrettes out of the other girls' hair ... and her brother was right behind her, mimicking her actions, doubling the trouble!

"Oh, God," I thought. "I can't do this!" My first instinct was to take a break and let someone else handle these two. But that felt too cowardly. So I picked up the girl and held her in my arms. She pulled at my glasses, tried to remove my earrings, clutched at my necklace—which reminded me that I should have removed the jewelry anyway before entering the nursery.

This child was fidgety, wanting to get down, then back up in my arms, then down again. She was frenzied, as if every nerve inside of her little body were plugged into an outlet. Finally, out of desperation, I held her close and began to pray aloud, as I walked around the nursery. I laid my hands on her back and asked God to calm her spirit. I felt a surge of compassion, and prayed even more for what was obviously the result of being born with drugs in her system. Remembering, too, that she was separated from her mother, I was overwhelmed by my own mothering instinct to protect her. I wanted nothing more than to soothe her with a mother's love.

Immediately, she calmed down. The other volunteers, who had witnessed this entire scenario, marveled at the sudden transformation, as did I. Her brother calmed down, too. I was able to hold her for the duration of the class, and we were able to teach our lesson.

When their father arrived, he had that questioning look that seemed to ask, "What trouble did they get into today?" We smiled, thanked him for trusting his children to us, and asked him to bring them back again.

Pray for your lessons. Pray for your students. Pray during class. Pray during the week. Imagine what ideas God will give us for our lessons if we take the time early in the week to ask him!

P ray intercessory prayers for your students.
R equest God's power in your classroom.
A sk the Holy Spirit, the "Teacher," for creative lesson ideas.
Y oke with a like-minded prayer partner.
E ntreat God to expel evil influences from the environment.
R emember that prayer works! So pray!

Goals and Objectives

As we pray, we need to ask two questions: What is the goal of our teaching? What is the objective of our lesson?

A good lesson is a treasure to be used again and again. We must plan our lessons so that our teaching is purposeful. Otherwise, it's like aiming an arrow without the slightest idea of where that arrow will land.

Goals give us the big picture. *Objectives* provide us with the steps to achieve our goals. It may take many steps to accomplish a single goal. For example, by teaching the book of Romans, our goal may be to teach the doctrines of the Christian faith. That's the big picture. As we actually begin our study of the first chapter of Romans, for example, our *objective* may be to teach the doctrine of sin (Rom. 1:18–32).

The goal of this book is to train teachers in the local church. The objective of this chapter is to help teachers design creative lessons through prayer, planning, and preparation.

The goal of our lives is heaven. Some life objectives are to worship God, fellowship with him through his Word, live holy, make disciples, be witnesses, love one another, be faithful husbands and wives, teach God's children, and shepherd God's people.

Looked at another way, objectives help us to accomplish our goals. The goal is the finish line. Objectives are the steps it takes to reach that finish line. For example, a goal may be to complete college. But the objective might be to simply get through one semester! Or, the objective might be to complete an application, enroll in school, or finish a class.

A goal may be to have a successful marriage. An objective might be to find a good wife. Other objectives might be to raise children who fear God, to keep a tidy home, or to learn how to cook.

Goals tell us what we want our teaching series to accomplish. Objectives tell us what we want to accomplish in each lesson of that series. With every met objective, we are on the way to accomplishing our goal.

The goal answers the question, "Why?" Why are we teaching what we are teaching? Objectives answer the question, "What?" What are we going to teach in this lesson to help us reach our goal?

Stating Goals

Clearly stated goals help to define objectives. As a rule, goals should be broad, but not too broad. The goal to "teach the Bible" is great for a lifetime but poorly stated for a six-week series.

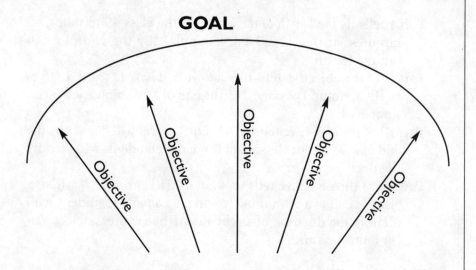

GOAL

OBJECTIVES

In general, goals should address topics or themes, books of the Bible, or Bible characters. For example, the goal for a six-month adult Bible study series can be one of the following:

- How to Raise Godly Children
- A Study Through the Book of John
- Courtship in the Book of Ruth

Writing Objectives

Most of us are clear with our goals in selecting the topics or books we want to teach. It's when we have to write down the objective that our purpose sometimes becomes a bit fuzzy.

There is perhaps nothing more frustrating than to listen to teachers who are all over the place with the lesson! They begin in Genesis and finish in Revelation, but in the end, the lesson has no point. Such lack of clarity results from not having clearly written objectives.

Frustrated, too, is the teacher who does not know what has actually been accomplished once the class has ended. An hour has been spent teaching, but what have the students actually learned? What has been deposited within them to help them grow? Has the lesson made a difference? Is God's purpose fulfilled?

Objectives give us a ruler by which we can measure our success. Each objective has four parts:

> **Part I** tells us *the length of the lesson.* Is the class 45 minutes, 50 minutes, or one hour? For example, "By the end of a 50-minute lesson . . ."
>
> **Part II** of the objective tells us *what we will have to teach.* It gives us the scriptural passage. "By the end of a 50-minute lesson on Romans 1, . . ."
>
> **Part III** of the objective tells us *what the student will know.* "By the end of a 50-minute lesson on Romans 1, students will identify the doctrine of sin . . ."
>
> **Part IV** of the objective tells us *what activity the teacher will use.* "By the end of a 50-minute lesson on Romans 1, students will identify the doctrine of sin by listing five expressions of sinful human nature."

Part I: Class Length

We will now view each part of the objective from a different angle. Part I of the lesson focuses on the amount of time that we have for the lesson. Remember that Jesus was sensitive to time. Good teachers don't allow the class session to run long simply because we are excited by our own lesson. When students sit too long, they may not return the following week. Always remember, too, that the length of the lesson depends on the age of our students.

Perhaps a more important concern is to be sure to start your class *on time.* Some teachers prefer to wait until more students arrive, but this can discourage those who have made the effort to arrive early. A good practice is to begin on time even if only one student is present. Since that individual made the effort to arrive promptly, begin teaching the class at the scheduled starting time. When others realize that the class will begin without them, they will be more apt to come on time.

Ending on time is also crucial. Remember that people may have had a long day at work, or they may have children to pick up from the baby-sitter or elderly parents to feed at home. Obviously, we can't teach everything in one night. The best teachers pay attention to time and honor others' schedules.

Part II: Scripture Passage

The Holy Spirit gives us guidance about what to teach. Because our primary curriculum is the Bible, every lesson must have a passage of Scripture as its reference. In other words, in Christian education our specific content is the Word of God. No objective is complete without reference to the Bible.

What if we are teaching a class that's centered on a theme such as parenting? Do we still need Scripture? The answer is "Yes!" The Bible provides us with principles for every area of our lives. It is the teacher's task to glean these biblical principles and apply them to our contemporary situation. This is what makes our education *Christian*.

Part III: Students' Knowledge

How well students are able to perform—or what they will know—depends primarily on the students' ages. Young children may only be able to repeat and memorize. Older students may be capable of writing a skit.

Bloom's Taxonomy, which gave us the "ladder" that we used to develop questions to ask in our lessons, helps us in selecting the right terms to use in writing our objective. Let's take another look.

Bloom's Taxonomy

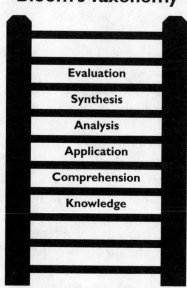

Evaluation

Synthesis

Analysis

Application

Comprehension

Knowledge

Part IV: Students' Activity

Teachers select activities that tell them whether or not the students have learned. In other words, we can evaluate how well we have taught when students are able to complete the task we've outlined in our objective.

For example, in a lesson on Genesis 1, the teacher may divide a junior high class and ask students to debate "Creation Versus Evolution." Younger children, like second graders, may study the same chapter, but instead of debating they may color pictures of the earth or animals.

Refer back to the activities on our list of "Show, Tell, Do" methods described in chapter 4 under "Masterful Methods." Remember to consider the students' age or developmental level before selecting the activity.

Has Learning Occurred?

Knowledge. If students can **recall**, the teacher will know that they have learned when students *repeat or answer who, what, when. where.*

Comprehension. If students can put the lesson **into their own words**, the teacher will know that students have learned when they *restate, describe, paraphrase, put into their own words, compare, contrast, explain the main idea.*

Application. If students can **choose one correct answer to solve a problem,** the teacher will know that students have learned when they *tell a Bible account selecting the right flannelgraph characters, make a selection, give one right answer, choose from several options, write and example, apply or organize information correctly.*

Analysis. If students can **identify reasons, motives, or causes,** the teacher will know that students have learned when they *answer the question Why?, debate, distinguish, analyze, identify reasons, look at causes, draw conclusions, find supporting evidence, identify motives.*

Synthesis. If students can **solve problems,** the teacher will know that students have learned when they *write their own story, complete this story, plan, design something original, develop, draw, find a solution, make an outline.*

Evaluation. If students can **judge**, the teacher will know that students have learned when they *decide which is better, give an opinion, agree or disagree, evaluate which is the best solution to a problem.*[1]

---

[1]Adapted from James M. Cooper, *Classroom Teaching Skills* (Lexington, MA: Heath, 1992).

Writing the Objective

Part I: **Amount.** How long is the class?
By the end of a lesson on . . .

Part II: **Account.** What is the Bible passage?
(Scripture reference)

Part III: **Ability.** What does the student have to know based on the taxonomy?
Students will be able to . . .

Part IV: **Activity.** How will the teacher know that the student has learned?
By . . .

Putting It All Together

Let's use a mnemonic or memory technique—alliteration—to help relate the new concepts in this chapter with information we've already discussed. Every objective should answer the following four questions:

Amount.   What is the amount of time for the lesson?
Account.   What is the scriptural reference for the lesson?
Ability.   What is the student expected to know?
Activity.   What activity has the teacher selected that will demonstrate that the student has learned?

Leader's Tip

Using the box above, ask students to practice writing an objective for a familiar passage such as Daniel 3:8–30—the account of Shadrach, Meshach, and Abednego. Place students into small groups to review their objectives. Each person should be able to answer the following questions about their classmate's lesson. Write these questions on the board or display on an overhead projector as discussion points:

1. If you were teaching this lesson, would you understand what you have to teach? Why or why not?

2. Are the *ability* and *activity* appropriate for the intended age group?

As with any learned skill such as biking, swimming, or public speaking, the key to writing objectives is practice, practice, practice. If you purchase curriculum, you have an idea of what to look for in well-planned objectives at the beginning of each lesson. If written correctly, objectives tell us exactly what we need to know to teach our lesson. Writing an objective is a vital part of a well-planned lesson.

The Lesson Plan

The table has been prepared. It's now time to serve the meal. Feeding and teaching are often used interchangeably to describe the process of spiritual nourishment that results from studying and learning the Word of God. After the goal and objective, the next step is the lesson plan. This is where we need the hamburger!

What Does a Hamburger Have to Do with Teaching?

How appropriate that the hamburger is our word picture for serving an absolutely scrumptious meal to our students! We've all heard of a BLT sandwich—bacon, lettuce, and tomato. Let me tempt your appetite with an HBLT—Hamburger, Bacon, Lettuce, and Tomato.

Hook, Book, Look, Took

Similar to serving a complete meal with soup, salad, entree, and dessert, the initial letters of Hamburger, Bacon, Lettuce, and Tomato represent each part of the lesson, that is, HBLT = Hook, Book, Look, Took.[2]

This four-step pattern helps us structure a lesson that guarantees effective teaching for everyone at every age. As we combine all of the

[2]Lawrence O. Richards, *Creative Bible Teaching* (Chicago: Moody Press, 1970), 107–14.

ingredients from the previous chapters, we can now discuss how to serve our meal.

Hooking the Students

When students arrive in your classroom, they bring with them the baggage of the day, and their experiences are as varied as are people themselves. The teacher's task is to focus students' attention to concentrate on the lesson at hand. Hooking students in the first few minutes of your lesson is essential.

Like the fisherman who reels in the fish for the day's catch, the Hook brings learners into one collective mindset. It is that part of the lesson that gets the students' attention.

The Hook should be so creative that it erases from students' minds whatever may have happened prior to walking into the classroom. Has a student had a bad day at school or work? Was it difficult to find a parking space? Did the baby-sitter arrive late? A creative Hook will help these concerns quickly fade from the learner's mind!

In addition to getting the students' attention, the Hook sets a goal. In effect, the Hook says, "This is what we will study today." With students' attention and the goal set, the Hook then leads naturally into the Bible lesson. Students are ready to learn!

Reel Them in Using . . .

Skits	Correspondence
Video Clips	Bible Quiz
Role-Play	Cartoons
Real-Life Situations	Drawings
Songs or Music	Open-ended Questions
Debate	Arts and Crafts
Agree/Disagree	Poetry
Current Affairs	Puppets
Panel Discussion	Flannelgraph
Controversial Topic	Pictures
No-Talk Teacher	Choral Reading
Games	Problem Solving
Interview	Personal Testimony
Read a Story	Flash Cards
Group Discussion	Collage
Drama Presentation	

Developing Hooks can be fun! But . . . there are some guidelines to follow for their use.[3]

The Ten Commandments of Hooks

1. The Hook must set the stage for the lesson.
2. The Hook must reel in the audience, getting their attention.
3. The Hook must inspire the class to desire more information.
4. The Hook must apply to the group you are teaching.
5. The Hook must relate to the Scripture passage.
6. The Hook must apply directly to the lesson.
7. The Hook must set a direction for the lesson.
8. The Hook must not put people to sleep.
9. The Hook must not offend people.
10. The Hook must not distract from the lesson.

The Bible Is the Book

The next part of the lesson is the Book, the Bible portion. Here, the Scripture passage is explained. Key to this part of the lesson itself is that the learners are actively engaged in acquiring the information. Remember, most people do not learn through the auditory channel, so the Book can be taught in other ways besides lecture. The teacher helps the learners understand the biblical information using a variety of methods, such as lecture, handouts, or question-and-answer.

A Contemporary Look

The Look portion of the lesson bridges the gap between Bible times and today. It helps learners look more intently at their contemporary circumstances. It's a close-up view, like looking through a magnifying glass at an aspect of their everyday lives.

The Look is a very important part of the lesson. Many teachers feel that once they have explained the Bible, they have taught. But that's not enough. Students must be able to apply what they have learned, and the Look helps transition learners from the scriptural context to their contemporary settings. Because it answers the question, "What's going on in our world today?" the Look helps learners relate biblical truth to life. As teachers, we guide students in this

---

[3]"The Ten Commandments of Hooks" is adapted from a student assignment.

process by helping them to look around at their family, their classmates, their church, their neighborhood, their community, their country, their world.

Taking the Took

In the Took portion, students are challenged to make decisions. Once they have looked at the broader picture, they are now better able to see how the lesson applies to them personally.

No lesson should end without students applying the information! If the lesson ends before this step, it stops too short! Students must be encouraged to respond to the Word of God, whether that response is in silent prayer, writing an action point, or walking forward in response to an invitation.

As teachers, we help students realize God's will for their lives. In this Took portion, we provide opportunity for acts of obedience.

For an overview of the Hook, Book, Look, Took concept see the following page.

Nook and Cook

Veteran teachers Wanda Parker and Dr. Shelly Cunningham have developed two additional portions of the lesson—Nook and Cook. With Larry Richards' Hook, Book, Look, and Took, the Nook and Cook make for a tasty meal.

According to Wanda Parker, the Nook is the devotional time that precedes the lesson. Prayer, praise, and worship help to soothe our learners' concerns and focus their attention on God. This turns their eyes upward, away from the distractions of the world, and brings an expectancy to receive exactly what they need from the Lord.

The Nook does not have to be lengthy and devotion methods can vary. It may include congregational singing, a tape playing, or a soloist or praise team. Prayer can be silent, two people praying together, corporate, or an individual who prays for the entire group.

According to Dr. Cunningham, the Cook occurs at the end of the lesson. Just as every restaurateur wants customers to leave with a satisfied palate and the desire to return, the teacher, having served the Word of God, wants students to come back the following week. Giving students a hint of what will happen next, asking an intriguing question with the promise to answer it the following week, or announcing an exciting topic that will be addressed in the coming session are ways to apply the Cook.

Hook  ...CAPTURES THE LEARNER'S *ATTENTION* AND SETS THE STAGE FOR THE LESSON. IT LEADS NATURALLY TO THE...

Book  ...THE *BIBLE* LESSON. LEARNERS ARE NOW READY TO DIG INTO THE WORD OF GOD TO PERSONALLY DISCOVER GOD'S TRUTH.

Look  ...FORMS A *BRIDGE* BETWEEN BIBLE TIMES AND TODAY. IT ANSWERS THE QUESTIONS, "WHAT IS HAPPENING IN THE WORLD AROUND US?" AND "HOW DOES THIS LESSON RELATE TO THE PEOPLE, EVENTS, OR CIRCUMSTANCES TODAY?"

Took  ...IS THE PERSONAL APPLICATION. STUDENTS MAKE DECISIONS BY RESPONDING TO THE QUESTION, "WHAT WILL I *DO* WITH WHAT I HAVE LEARNED?"

Sample Lessons

See appendix A for examples of lessons that have been written and taught by students and volunteer teachers in the local church. These lessons demonstrate how to use Hook, Book, Look, and Took and will help you design your own creative lessons.

Purchasing Curriculum

Writing our own lessons is one way to meet the cultural needs of the people to whom we minister. But it's not the only way. There are also excellent publishing houses that write and develop curriculum for individual ministries to purchase. Here are some special points to consider when selecting materials for the people you teach.

Curriculum with the Bible verses printed directly onto the page is convenient and easy to use, but it may discourage students from actually reading the Bible. Always encourage your students to read directly from the Word of God. We don't want them to assume that the Bible is too difficult to understand. Use versions that are appropriate for the age group you are teaching.

If curriculum is illustrated, select curriculum with pictures that accurately reflect the ethnic and cultural identity of the people to whom you minister. Children need to see pictures of children who look like them in the material they read so that they grow in their God-esteem. During a time of questioning and reevaluation, teenagers need to be reassured that the Bible speaks to their culture, too. And unfortunately, with the reality of societal pressures and prejudice, adults also need to see pictures of people from their own ethnic group. The publisher's cultural sensitivity is often reflected in the illustrations and drawings in the curricula. This is an important area that is not to be overlooked.

The checklist on the following page may be helpful in providing additional guidelines for selecting curriculum for your children's church, Sunday school, Bible study class, or discipleship ministry.

Prepare Early in the Week

Whether studying curriculum or writing your own lesson, one important rule is this—prepare early in the week. Waiting until Saturday night before a Sunday morning class allows no time for you to adequately pray or plan. Finding materials and selecting activities to bring your lesson alive is easier if you begin early.

Curriculum Evaluation Checklist

Ten Questions to Ask Yourself

❏ 1. Do both students and teachers use their Bibles?

❏ 2. Is the Bible presented in a historically accurate framework?

❏ 3. Does the curriculum address the need for a personal relationship with Jesus Christ?

❏ 4. Are objectives clearly stated and measurable?

❏ 5. Does the curriculum address the cultural needs of the students?

❏ 6. Do the lessons address the real challenges of your students?

❏ 7. Are the methods varied so that you can teach students who learn through the auditory, visual, or kinesthetic channel?

❏ 8. Do the lessons allow for students to be actively involved?

❏ 9. Is the curriculum appropriate for the students' age?

❏ 10. Are the pictures and illustrations visually attractive?

*Allowing one point for each question, if the curriculum scores below 8 points, keep looking! You **will** find the one that's right for your ministry.*

When should you start to prepare? Monday morning or evening, during your daily time with the Lord, is a good time to begin. After a brief overview, you can take a few minutes Tuesday through Saturday to read through portions of the lesson. This way you are studying each day! And during lunchtime or even when heading for the supermarket, you might see that one special little item that's just perfect to help with an activity. God can speak to your heart and direct your steps to find the materials you need if you give him—and yourself—adequate time.

Do You Remember?

In this chapter, we evaluated the importance of prayer, planning, and preparation in designing lessons. Here is a summary of the major points to remember.

- *The Prayer Channel.* The first step in lesson planning is to pray. God gives inspiration. There is power in prayer. Remember the acrostic, PRAYER: Pray intercessory prayers for your students. Release God's power in your classroom. Ask the Holy Spirit, the "Teacher," for creative lesson ideas. Yoke with a like-minded prayer partner. Entreat God to keep away evil influences from the environment. Remember that prayer works! So pray!
- *Goals and Objectives.* Goals give us the *big* picture. Objectives provide us with the *steps*.
- *Stating Goals.* Clearly stated goals help to define objectives.
- *Writing Objectives.* Objectives give us a ruler by which to measure our success. Each objective has four parts: class length, Scripture passage, students' knowledge, students' activity, or Amount, Account, Ability, Activity.
- *The Lesson Plan.* Hook, Book, Look, Took are the main parts of the lesson. Cook and Nook are additional ingredients that round out the "meal."
- *Purchasing Curriculum.* Curriculum should reflect the cultural and ethnic identity of the learner. Evaluate with the Curriculum Evaluation Checklist.
- *Prepare Early in the Week.* Allow God—and yourself—time to develop the lesson. Begin early. Saturday night is too late!

Cook: Age-appropriate Teaching

In the next chapter, we will examine specific ways to teach children in the nursery and preschool and children in grades kindergarten through 6. We will also make suggestions for arranging the environment and discuss how to discipline.

Chapter 7

Lo! Children!
Teaching Children from Nursery to Sixth Grade

Objective

By the end of this chapter, judge the merits of teaching developmentally by evaluating the needs of children in the nursery, preschool, kindergarten, and grades 1 through 6.

It's easy to spot a church that is dying. There simply are no children there.

What a Blessing!

Boundless bundles of energy, activity, and excitement, children are a blessing to every family . . . and to every church.

> Lo, children are an heritage of the LORD, and the fruit of the womb is his reward. As arrows are in the hand of a mighty man; so are children of the youth. Happy is the man that hath his quiver full of them: they shall not be ashamed, but they shall speak with the enemies in the gate.
>
> —PSALM 127:3–5 KJV

Happy is the man . . . happy, fortunate, too, is the pastor who has his quiver full of children! With these little ones come parents, grandparents, godparents, aunts, uncles, and cousins. Children are part of families, and it takes families to build churches.

Like riches left to descendants, God gives us children as heirlooms. Regardless of the circumstances of birth, every child is born on purpose—God's purpose. With a biblical foundation, children become the spiritual legacy through which we bless the next generation.

In the Psalms passage above, God gives us a picture of a strong person with a full quiver—a case that holds arrows. Whether in offense or defense, arrows are effective missiles. Aiming an arrow involves the whole person. Feet are braced. Arms confidently cradle the bow. The mind is alert, ready to respond to every rustle of a leaf or snap of a branch. Eyes are focused for any glimpse of the opponent.

Like shooting an arrow, we must be totally involved with our children, confident in the ability of God's Word to shape and mold their character, alert to the world's tricks that would derail their purpose, responsive to our children's needs, and focused in providing relevant Christian education. When we arm our children with the Word of God, when we weave the truths of Scripture into their very fiber, when their thoughts are centered on obedience and worship, our children fulfill their purpose and thereby strike a blow at the very heart of the enemy, Satan.

What is the goal of Christian education for infants, toddlers, and children? How do we teach so that we meet their needs? As always, Jesus provides us with the model.

Wisdom, Stature, and Favor

The Bible gives us few details about Jesus as a child, but the glimpse we do have of the Savior when he was 12 is big enough to set a standard for children's ministries.

> And Jesus grew in wisdom and stature, and in favor with God and men. —LUKE 2:52

Jesus grew in wisdom, which speaks of his intellectual or cognitive development. Jesus also grew in stature and in favor. Stature represents health and physical development. Favor with God speaks of Christ's spiritual development, while favor with men refers to his social development. Jesus was well-balanced!

In Christian education, our goal is to help our children grow. Children grow on a spiritual foundation (Luke 2:52). The acrostic GROW forms a mission statement for children's ministries.

G iving love to children by
R elating to their needs and teaching them
O bedience to the
W ord, will, and way of God

Giving Love

The first letter in the acrostic GROW is for giving love. People who work with children must genuinely love them. The work is difficult, the hours long, and the rewards often intangible. Grouchy, angry, irritable workers who are short on patience need not apply! Only those who manifest the fruit of the Spirit should consider children's work.

> But the fruit of the Spirit is love, joy, peace, patience, kindness, goodness, faithfulness, gentleness and self-control.
>
> —GALATIANS 5:22

Here is the evidence of being born again. It's like describing a peach. The peach is fuzzy, sweet, yellow, orange, soft, firm, delicious, chewy, and ripe. Each quality describes an aspect of one fruit, the peach. We cannot isolate a quality, like yellow, for instance, and say that we have the peach. Not until we have all nine qualities do we have a peach.

So, too, it is with salvation. There is only *one* fruit of the Spirit. Its nine aspects are all part of the same fruit. Either we have all of it, or we have none of it. Where there is no fruit, there is no evidence of the Spirit of God, and without the Spirit, we are none of his (Rom. 8:9)!

Being saved, being born again, is mandatory for everyone who works with children. It is the primary requirement. We cannot expect love, joy, peace, patience, kindness, goodness, faithfulness, gentleness, and self-control—qualities essential in children's ministry—to emanate from persons who are under the control of the enemy.

Even when saved, not everyone is fit to work with children. Before committing themselves, new volunteers should engage in the following process to see if ministering to children is definitely where God has called them to work.

- Volunteer for one month. During this time assist with handing out supplies, playtime, cleanup, providing snacks, reading, and other tasks.
- The new volunteer should now participate with a veteran teacher in preparing lessons to understand the process.
- Teach part of the lesson for one or two weeks. Ask the veteran teacher for feedback.
- Teach an entire lesson under the watchful eyes of the veteran teacher. Ask for feedback.
- You're on your own! Pray, plan, and prepare. Teach knowing that the Holy Spirit is your helper.

Teachers and volunteers should come dressed for service! Wear a warm, gracious smile and comfortable clothing. Heels and stockings, jewelry and dresses, are ill-suited for crawling around the floor, changing diapers, and rocking children to sleep. So, too, are suits, white shirts, and ties! Rubber-soled shoes, skirts, comfortable slacks or jeans and a T-shirt are perfect attire for the wear and tear of hands-on ministry.

Relating to Their Needs

The second letter in the acrostic GROW is for relating to the needs of babies and children. Understanding how infants, toddlers, and children develop helps us to minister to them more effectively.

Nursery: Infants and Toddlers

For infants and toddlers from birth to three years old, developing motor skills is a major task. Learning how to grasp or hold objects, learning how to crawl, stand, and walk, and learning how to talk are

Leader's Tip

Children's ministries are usually the ministries most in need of workers. Often we assume that everyone who volunteers to teach children is saved, but this fact is *not* to be taken for granted. A detailed application will give us the information we need to evaluate the veracity of the salvation experience. See the "Volunteer's Application" and "Letter of Commitment" in appendix B as an example of what to ask potential children's workers, teachers, and volunteers.

Loving Guidelines

Because of the times in which we live, teachers and volunteers need to be given guidelines on how to express affection to the children. Any violation is grounds to remove a volunteer from the children's ministry.

- Always hug children from the *side,* with your arm around the shoulder. It's called the "A-frame hug." Never hug children facing front. Touch *hands to shoulders* only.
- Never *kiss* a child! Never, never, never!
- Never *hit* or *spank* a child! Employ time-outs for behavior problems or return the child to his or her parent.
- Never *call children names,* like "stupid," or jokingly put them down. And don't allow children to call one another names, either.
- Always take children to the restroom accompanied by a *fellow teacher.* An adult should never be alone with a child.

important milestones in the young lives of babies. These children are very active, and therefore require much supervision. A ratio of one adult per three or four children ensures that every child has the help he or she needs.

Infants and toddlers are sensitive and easily frightened. Some types of stuffed animals or puppets are more likely to alarm rather than amuse small children. They experience separation anxiety when it's time for their parents to leave, and usually they cry until they have been sufficiently distracted by an activity. Parents who are bringing their children to the nursery for the first time should remain with them until the child feels comfortable enough for them to leave. A rocking chair or two in the nursery is a wonderful way of calming and soothing any crying child.

For babies and toddlers, learning is most effective through play and least effective with lecture. Preaching to children, common in some cultures, does not result in learning. Activity is the way to teach infants. They love songs that involve hand movements, and they enjoy jumping up and down and clapping their hands. Children also enjoy hearing the same Bible account or singing the same song over and over and over.

Teaching Babies

Since babies are capable of learning and remembering, a regular class routine is important. For example, begin the morning with reading as children enter the nursery. The morning has been busy with their parents rushing to get them dressed and fed (yes, ask parents to feed their children before bringing them to class!), so children may be as out of breath when they arrive as are the adults.

Be sure to place a color-coded name tag on the upper part of the back. For example, eighteen-month-old children may wear yellow, two-year-olds green, and three-year-olds red. Next, invite children to get a toy or take a book from the shelf and sit them with their age group—eighteen-month-old children in one circle, two-year-olds in a different circle, and three-year-olds in another circle.

After everyone is settled and playtime or reading time is over, assist the children in putting back the toys or books. As they return to their section of the classroom, begin singing songs, or have a video-tape of Christian songs playing so that children can sing along.

Following this praise and worship time, children can now learn a short Bible lesson. Because little ones are only able to pay attention for about three minutes, lessons must be short and related to every activity of the morning. Color, voices, and motion will hold their attention.

Tell Bible accounts using puppets or flannelgraph. When using flannelgraph, remove the characters from within the pages of the Bible itself so that children will know this is God's Word. The toddlers can even place the flannelgraph onto the board once they are familiar with the Bible account.

Puppets, Reading, and Snack Time

With puppets, make sure that children don't see them unless they are on the hand. According to professionals who specialize in training puppeteers to minister in the local church, children become disappointed if they see the puppets lifeless and motionless. Hide the puppets behind drapes or screens once they make their exit. Puppets are an effective teaching method and an exciting way to tell a Bible account.

Here is an important note: Saying Bible "account" is more accurate than saying Bible "story." Stories are what we see on television, and they are not real. On the contrary, everything that occurred in the Bible is true! We are learning actual accounts of what happened.

Reading to children, of course, is another way of teaching them. Show them the pictures and ask the children to point out objects, tell what colors they see, name the objects, or repeat the teacher's words. In this way, they are learning by being actively involved in the lesson.

Snack time is an important time, too. Remember, Jesus fed his followers. Young children are often hungry, so providing juice and sugar-free crackers is a must. Creative teachers will build upon the lesson by making this time an extension of what the children are learning.

Review, Reward

Before children are returned to their parents, take the time to reinforce the lesson. Ask review questions. Children love praise, and they love to be rewarded. Clapping your hands when they've repeated correctly, giving them stickers on the backs of their hands, or giving treats are wonderful ways of making their class time enjoyable.

Briefly explain the lesson to parents, or give them a handout so that they can reinforce the Bible lesson at home. The following is teacher Rebecca Hedgepath's nursery schedule that coincides with a two-hour church service.

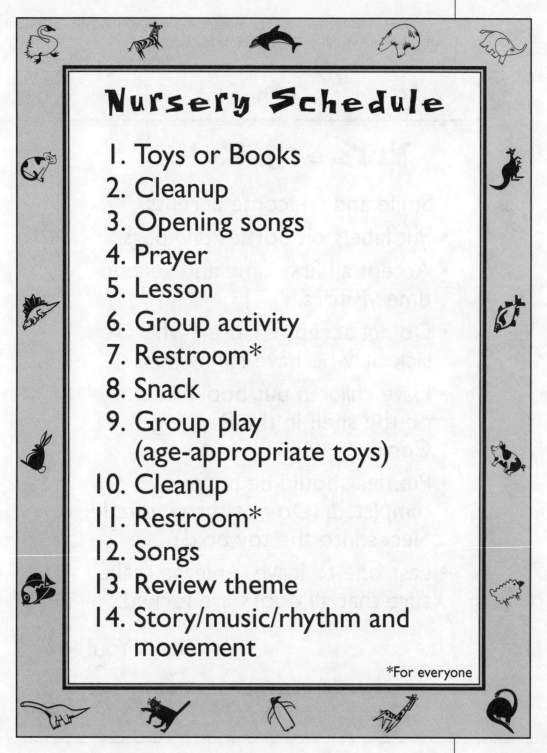

Nursery Schedule

1. Toys or Books
2. Cleanup
3. Opening songs
4. Prayer
5. Lesson
6. Group activity
7. Restroom*
8. Snack
9. Group play
   (age-appropriate toys)
10. Cleanup
11. Restroom*
12. Songs
13. Review theme
14. Story/music/rhythm and
    movement

*For everyone

Nursery rules may vary from ministry to ministry. Post rules so that they are visible to all. A sample follows.

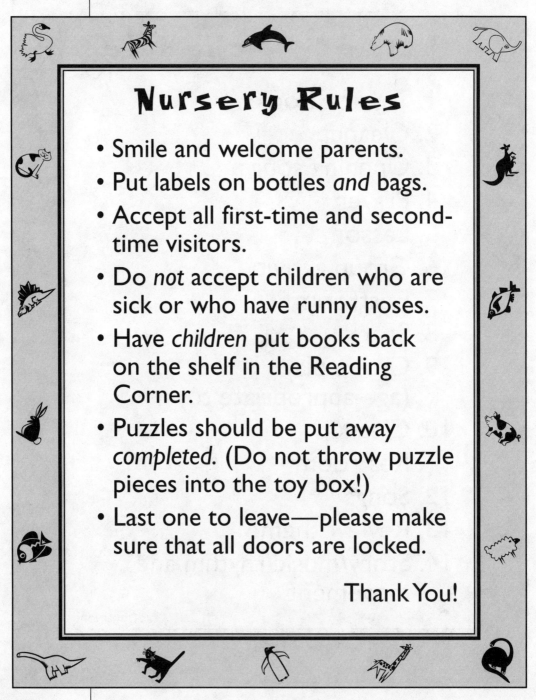

Nursery Rules

- Smile and welcome parents.
- Put labels on bottles *and* bags.
- Accept all first-time and second-time visitors.
- Do *not* accept children who are sick or who have runny noses.
- Have *children* put books back on the shelf in the Reading Corner.
- Puzzles should be put away *completed.* (Do not throw puzzle pieces into the toy box!)
- Last one to leave—please make sure that all doors are locked.

Thank You!

Be Safe and Sanitize

Remember, too, that because they are learning about the world around them, infants are interested in every little detail on their eye level. Take preventive measures such as covering sockets with plastic protectors and removing small items that may find their way into the mouths of babies. Here are a few extra tips:

- Avoid using safety pins or paper clips in the nursery.
- Toys should be sanitized regularly, sheets changed weekly, and carpets and throw rugs cleaned as often as necessary.
- Wear rubber gloves when changing diapers.
- Wash hands thoroughly and regularly.
- Children who are ill, coughing, or with runny noses should not be allowed to remain in the nursery.
- If children have allergies, parents should notify the volunteers and remind them weekly so that their child is not given any food or juice other than what the parent provided.
- If children need to be given medication, nursery workers should not accept them. It is unwise to give this responsibility to volunteers.

One Service, One Sunday, Once a Month

Parents should be encouraged to volunteer in the nursery and preschool. In most ministries, additional help is necessary, and dads and moms fulfill their responsibility to their children and to the workers by volunteering at least one service one Sunday once a month. Most parents willingly comply.

Parents must sign in when dropping off their child and sign out when picking up their children. Check signatures! All bags, bottles,

Leader's Tip

An excellent resource that makes it easy to train your staff and volunteers in safety and sanitation measures is *Sanitation and Hygiene in Church Child Care*. To order, contact:

Church Risk Management, Inc.
P.O. Box 1017
Lake Wales, FL 33859-1017
(941) 676-7808

and clothing should be clearly labeled. Have blank labels available for parents who have rushed out of the house forgetting this important step. Discourage parents from sending children to the nursery with personal toys. This will help avoid tugs-of-war between children.

In large churches with limited nursery capacity, the children of parents who have volunteered should be received into the nursery *first*. If there is a line, bring these parents out of the line to the front. Or, have a separate line for regular volunteers as well as for those who have volunteered within the past month. First, sign in the parents who have volunteered before attending to the others. This *visual* will teach parents that there is a reward for service. (See appendix B for the "Nursery Sign-In.")

Preschool and Kindergarten: Four- and Five-Year-Olds

Many of the principles listed above also relate to preschool and kindergarten children. Because they are older, motor skills, coordi-

Leader's Tip

The "Nursery Rules" and "Nursery Schedule" will serve to remind your workers of what you expect of them. In addition, consider the following bits of practical advice.

Check Attitudes, Rotate Volunteers

Attitude is so important when working with children. Rotating volunteers to avoid burnout is essential in maintaining a staff that is cordial. Being too tired makes for a grumpy volunteer. Look out for the needs of your staff and make sure that there are Sundays when they are able to attend church service.

Give Tapes

Parents and volunteers feel especially appreciated when given free tapes of the morning service. Include this expense in your annual budget, or find some other way to reward your workers.

The Break Room

Remember that Jesus fed people! When the classrooms are adequately supervised, invite teachers to take breaks by having a "break room" set up with coffee, juice, and snacks.

nation, and verbal skills are improved. Also, children in this age group are becoming better at movement and memory. A little more independent than at the earlier stages, they don't experience as much separation anxiety and are more familiar with the classroom setting.

Preschoolers need less adult-to-child supervision, but a reasonable ratio still needs to be maintained. One worker for every five or six children may be sufficient. Still very active, these children need to be guided in their play, taught to share, and encouraged to solve disputes without fighting.

At this age, learning is most effective through play. Group and individual games and activities teach them how to share and cooperate with others. These children can sit a little longer than nursery children, but they still should not be expected to sit for too long. They enjoy the same variety of activities, including flannelgraph and puppets, books with lots of pictures, arts and crafts, and dressing up as Bible characters.

Children at this age have vivid imaginations, and it may be difficult for them to separate fantasy from reality. The past and future become blurred because children are aware only of today. So the story preschoolers may tell might seem like a "lie," but these children are not intentionally trying to deceive. They do, however, understand the difference between telling the truth and telling a lie. In general, remember that these children have vivid imaginations.

Activity Centers

Because their attention spans are still very short—only five or ten minutes—one excellent way to teach the preschooler is to arrange the room into activity centers. This allows movement from one area of the room to another. Each time the activity changes, children are learning the same Bible account but through a different method. With ample volunteers, activity centers are a refreshing way to teach, and setting them up is easy.

Designate one area of the classroom as the reading corner. During the course of the morning, children may wander over to listen to a Bible account where an adult is seated on the floor (always at eye level with the children) reading about Noah's ark, for example. In another portion of the room, puppets may be acting out the same Bible account of Noah that is being read in the reading corner. In a third part of the classroom, children may be engaged in arts and crafts, like drawing or coloring the animals that went into the ark. And in a fourth area of the room, students may sit and have snacks like animal crackers and juice. At the start of class, children can sit together for age-appropriate praise and worship before being "dismissed" to the activity centers.

In a classroom like this, it may seem as if there is too much commotion for children to actually learn, but this is not the case. Preschoolers are spontaneous and are constantly moving. With the classroom organized for their developmental level, children are encouraged to gravitate to the activity that best mirrors their learning style. The bonus is that as they hear the lesson in different ways, reinforcement is occurring. Careful planning makes for an exciting, engaging experience for teachers, volunteers, and students.

Pleasing the teacher is a major focus of small children. Remember to reward children with stickers and stars to encourage learning.

For a more traditional class time, adapt the nursery class schedule and post the same rules. (See appendix B for sign-in sheets for preschool and kindergarten.)

Grades 1–3

By grades 1, 2, and 3, children are in primary school where they are learning how to read and write. Their muscles are still developing, so holding pencils, crayons, and scissors is still a bit awkward. Among children, development occurs at different rates, and their skill levels may be as varied as are the children themselves. Volunteers should be available to help children complete tasks so that the children feel successful.

Cooperative learning is effective with primary children, so group activities like plays and games are favorites among this age group. Since they are learning how to communicate, children enjoy talking. Lessons that encourage children to answer questions or to talk with one another are smart ways to teach.

Love, acceptance, and security are very special needs of young children. A warm, supportive classroom with teachers who see the best in them rather than their errors and mistakes is a wonderful teaching-learning environment. To applaud and nurture young children, try new and different tasks to give them confidence and encouragement. Because six- to eight-year-old children are still so young, be sure to have parents sign in when dropping off and sign out when picking up their children. (See appendix B for the "Children's Church Sign-In.")

Grades 4–6

As children continue to develop in grades 4, 5, and 6, they become increasingly competitive. They love games and receiving rewards, such as having stars next to their name on a wall chart. Don't play favorites! If children feel that they have been treated unfairly, they may easily become discouraged, and tempers may flare.

Perhaps most important for this age group is to remember that children this age and younger perceive their world in concrete terms. In other words, young children are not yet able to think in the abstract or think hypothetically. For example, to talk to an elementary school-age child about "walking with God" does not mean what it means to an adult. For young children, walking with God literally means to walk, as in physically putting one foot in front of the other and taking step after step. They are not able to connect the abstract phrase "walking with God" with living the Christian life.

Because children are in this literal stage, some Christian terms may be confusing for them. Asking Jesus to "come into their heart," for instance, may not be the best way to offer salvation. Imagine asking someone to actually break through the chest cavity to enter the heart! Instead, asking "Jesus to be their best friend" or asking him to be "Savior" (and explain what the word *Savior* means) is a better way of inviting children to be born again. In general, avoid using Christian clichés when teaching.

Children this age identify with role models and are fascinated with heroes. They have great empathy for people who may have problems and are eager to do whatever they can to help. Children can also be cruel to one another, pointing out every fault or laughing at every mistake. Less accepting of differences, children need to be taught how to be kind to others who do not look, speak, or act as they do.

During these years, boys prefer activities with boys, and girls prefer being with girls. Joining clubs and playing on teams is very attractive to them, so it's easy to see how young children can be influenced to join gangs. Church groups, teams, and clubs are important alternatives.

Obedience

The third letter in the acrostic GROW is obedience. Teaching children obedience to God and to their parents is central to helping them grow. How we discipline in the church setting helps children learn that sin has consequences and there are rewards for right actions.

Helping children to be obedient is every teacher's goal. Together, students and teacher should discuss the classroom rules. Also, discuss the consequences for disobedience. Post rules in the classroom, refer to them often, and enforce the rules. Teacher Demetra Pearson suggests writing rules in positive rather than in negative terms. For example, rather than saying, "Don't hit," or "No fighting," offer children positive alternatives.

- Speak to one another nicely.
- Raise your hand to ask or answer a question.
- Walk in the halls.
- Chew gum only before or after class.

In general, teachers who arrive in their classroom early and who have prepared their lesson well tend to experience less discipline problems among the children. Having a sense of humor helps us not to take every offense personally.

Discipline

When children are disobedient, giving a time-out—one minute for each year of the child's age—is an effective way to discipline. If the child is two, then the time-out should last no longer than two minutes. If the child is ten, then the time-out should last no longer than ten minutes. Ask the child to sit in a designated spot or stand in front of the child to enforce the time-out.

It's important to welcome children back into the group with words that inspire good behavior. Teachers should also discover ways to help children cooperate. Be quick to notice when they do something correctly, and comment on this improvement to the rest of the class. Remember, children *want* to behave.

Parents should be notified if their child has a discipline problem that continues to disrupt the class. In some instances, children may need to be returned to their parents who are in the church service. Of course, walking into the sanctuary with a child is distracting, so such action is reserved for only the severest of cases. Some churches have a pager system for summoning parents, and this is an effective way of being able to contact them in a hurry.

Word, Will, Way of God

"W," the final letter in the acrostic GROW, centers on teaching children the Word, will, and way of God. Sunday school or children's chufch are the settings where children learn the Word of God on their developmental level.

Children's Church

Sunday school and children's church are distinctly different. If Sunday school meets before the church service, children are usually expected to sit in the main church service afterward with their parents.

Children's church differs in that it takes place at the same time that adult worship occurs. Parents sign their children in to their respective classrooms before heading to service. After the children have gathered, teachers and volunteers lead the children to one general area where all classes meet together for praise and worship.

Here, children collect their own offering, pray for one another, and in general conduct a "service" where they are the leaders. During this time, a teacher may review the previous month's curriculum. On First Sunday, some churches may even have a special treat such as a drill team that marches and recites rhymes of what the children have been studying. After this gathering, children return to their individual classrooms for an in-depth lesson, crafts, or snacks.

As mentioned earlier, lessons are to be Bible-centered. Children should read Scripture from their Bibles rather than from curriculum books. While the latter is convenient, children may become accustomed to *not* reading their Bibles.

Curriculum should also be culturally appropriate. It may be confusing for children to see pictures of Jesus and understand that he loves them if Jesus does not resemble them. Memorizing Scripture should be emphasized and rewarded. All children should know these fundamental passages:

- The Ten Commandments
- Psalm 23
- The Lord's Prayer
- The Armor of God
- The Fruit of the Spirit

A *spiral curriculum* presents a lesson from the same biblical passage for every grade level. Lessons are developmentally appropriate and target the needs of each age group. As children progress, information they learned in earlier grades is repeated again in later grades but with more detail. The spiral curriculum is excellent! It reintroduces and reinforces previously learned material and is an excellent way to help children remember.

Salvation and Baptism

At the close of every class, children should be encouraged to accept Jesus Christ as their Savior.

"Let the little children come to me, and do not hinder them, for the kingdom of heaven belongs to such as these." —MATTHEW 19:14

One way to do this is to say a short prayer that all of the children can understand and ask them to repeat the prayer. Because they know the difference between right and wrong, children have a keen awareness of sin. They want to please God. And they want to be saved. In every class, give them this opportunity.

A Child's Salvation Prayer

Dear Heavenly Father,

Thank you for sending Jesus to die for me. I am sorry for my sins. Thank you for forgiving me. I ask Jesus to be my friend and Savior. In the name of the Father, Son, and Holy Spirit, Amen.

Baptizing Children

In our church ministry, we personally talk to every child who asks to be baptized. We find out whether the child is aware of sin by asking if he or she has ever done anything wrong. While we don't tell children that they are "bad," children who cannot admit that they have done something wrong may be too young to understand the true meaning of salvation. Awareness of sin is a prerequisite for salvation.

Children are encouraged to explain their experience with God in their own words. If the child does not understand, it is suggested to parents that they wait until their child is older before being baptized. All too often, anxious moms and dads urge their child into the baptismal pool for tradition's sake. This is discouraged because, unfortunately, these children will ask to be "rebaptized" as adults because they did not understand what they did as children. An objective voice can help the parent understand the importance of waiting until the child is ready. Recently, one of our volunteers, Janice Webb, related the following experience.

In keeping with our policy for all children who are to be baptized, a mother set up an appointment with me and brought her son. During our talk, she sat at the edge of her chair as I asked her child some questions.

This little boy understood who Jesus was, but when I asked if he had accepted Jesus as his Savior, tears welled in his eyes. "No," he said. I asked if he wanted to ask Jesus to be his Savior now. He hesitated, feeling the pressure from his mom. Tears flowed. "No," he whimpered. I assured him that God appreciates us when we are honest with him and told him to talk to me when he was ready. His mother seemed very disappointed, but I urged her to be patient and to allow the Holy Spirit to work in her son's life.

This past Easter during children's church, this little boy came running down the hall looking for me. "I'm ready to ask Jesus to be my Savior," he announced. We prayed together, and I could sense his sincerity. This time, I cried. When his mother came to pick him up from class, I told her what had happened, and then *she* cried. I thanked her for being patient and for allowing her son to make this important decision in his own time and without pressure.

Because of their stage of development, children may not be able to understand that baptism is like being buried with Jesus Christ and being raised with him in the newness of life. Understanding such symbolism, however, is not vital. Once children have prayed and are able to answer the following questions, they are ready for baptism.

1. Who is Jesus?
2. Have you ever done anything wrong?
3. Have you asked God to forgive you?
4. Is Jesus your Savior? Do you want him to be your Best Friend?
5. If you do something wrong today, is he still your Friend?

Baptism and First Communion

Children's baptism and First Communion are the ordinances that follow confession of Jesus Christ as Savior. Because baptism and Communion are major events in the lives of believers, sensitive parents will wait until their children understand the significance of both and express the desire to be baptized. (When Communion is served, because they think they are snacks, children are usually eager to eat the bread or crackers and drink the juice, which should be gently discouraged by both pastor and parents.)

Christian education classes that teach the meaning of these ordinances are helpful for the entire family. Adults are given information and are taught how to answer their children's questions, and children are taught in terms they can understand. After parents and children attend two one-hour classes to learn about baptism and the Lord's Supper, the children are baptized and receive Communion at a special evening service during the Easter season.

According to a former student of mine who is an educational director at a large multicultural church in California, First Communion Sunday is a favorite among the entire church community. In addition to tracking those children who are saved during the year, First Communion Sunday meets the needs of families who want a ceremony to remember these special times in their children's lives.

Children are first baptized in a special service. Then, at a designated point during the evening service on First Communion Sunday, parents join their children at the front of the church near the altar where they administer the bread and juice to their children.

It's a spectacular sight! Children—most of them dressed in white—taking Communion from their parents! It's a moment that neither will ever forget. (See appendix B for information on First Communion.)

A Firm Foundation

Ministry to children—and their parents—is so important. Here we build a firm foundation for a life committed to the Father. What an opportunity to train future pastors, teachers, preachers, missionaries,

Leader's Tip

Ask your teachers to complete the following assignment: Based on what we have studied about the needs of children in nursery, preschool, kindergarten, and children in first to sixth grade, complete the chart "What Do Children Need to Know About ...?"

At each age, what should we teach children about the Father, Jesus Christ, the Holy Spirit, the Bible, and the church? Note your ideas in the corresponding boxes on the chart.

What Do Children Need to Know About . . . ?

	The Father	Jesus Christ	The Holy Spirit	The Bible	The Church
Nursery					
Preschool					
Kindergarten					
1st–3rd Grade					
4th–6th Grade					

evangelists, and ministers! We never know who the young child will grow to become, so we must see every child as sent to us by God and use every opportunity to teach with excellence.

Often ministry to children seems to be the hardest work with the least benefits. Few senior pastors see those people who work behind the scenes. Teachers don't see the immediate results of their labor, so it's easy to become discouraged. Wise pastors, directors, and superintendents will take every opportunity to celebrate and encourage these volunteers. "Thank you" dinners at Christmas and special occasions, like church-sponsored summer retreats, help keep motivation high.

A Note on Decorating

Children feel important to God when their classroom environment is bright, cheerful, comfortable, and neat. Decorate classrooms with Christian images and with children's storybook characters and animals. Small, colorful chairs and tables, bright toy boxes, racks for coats and sweaters, and artwork at children's eye level affirm to children—and to their parents—that they are valued.

Do You Remember?

In this chapter we judged the merits of teaching developmentally by evaluating the needs of children in nursery through sixth grade. Here is a summary of major points to remember.

- *Children Are a Blessing.* A church without children is a dying church, so cherish all of the children in your ministry. Deposit God's Word in their hearts by teaching on their age level using games and fun activities.
- *Growing in Wisdom, Stature, and Favor.* Children GROW on a spiritual foundation according to Luke 2:52. Therefore, we Give love to children by Relating to their needs and teaching them Obedience to the Word, will, and way of God. This is the purpose of children's ministry.
- *Giving Love.* Volunteers must genuinely love children and exhibit the fruit of the Spirit. Affection to children must be expressed appropriately. Hug side-to-side—the A-frame hug—and touch hands to shoulder only.

- *Relating to Their Needs.* Understanding children developmentally means that we are able to minister to them more effectively.

  Nursery. Children are very active and require much supervision. Maintaining a ratio of one adult per three or four children is vital. Children learn through play, puppets, singing, reading, and repetition, and they love receiving rewards such as stickers.

  Preschool and Kindergarten. Although older and a bit more independent, these children also need a lot of supervision. One adult worker for every five or six children is recommended. These children also learn through play, and they have vivid imaginations. Activity centers are an excellent way to teach children of this age.

  Grades 1–3. Development occurs at different rates for different children. Since their muscles are still developing, volunteers should help children complete tasks so that the children feel successful. Cooperative learning, question-and-answer, and a warm, supportive learning environment are effective ways to teach.

  Grades 4–6. At this age, children are increasingly competitive. Playing games are excellent activities, and awarding prizes are great motivators. These children are still in the literal stage and have difficulty grasping abstract concepts. In general, avoid using Christian clichés when teaching.

- *Obedience.* Discipline is important to teach children obedience. Employ time-outs—a maximum of one minute for every year of the child's age—when problems occur. Notify parents when necessary.

- *Word, Will, and Way of God.* Children's church is one way to teach children the Word of God. The children conduct a church service complete with praise and worship where they are the leaders. Afterward they divide into smaller classes for an in-depth lesson, crafts, and snacks. The spiral curriculum, which presents a lesson from the same biblical passage for every grade level, reintroduces information at various stages and is an excellent way to reinforce previously learned material.

- *Salvation and Baptism.* In every class, children should be invited to accept Jesus Christ as their Friend and Savior. They should be baptized and receive Communion only when they understand what these ordinances mean. First Communion Sunday during the Easter season is one way to mark these special times both for children and their parents.
- *Decorate.* A cheerful environment is important to children. Decorate rooms with biblical themes or with characters and animals with which they are familiar. Small chairs and tables suitable for children and artwork at eye level affirm to children and their parents that they are valued.

What's Cooking?

As children become older, their needs become more complex, and Christian education must vary accordingly. In the next chapter we will discuss how to meet the needs of that very special group—pre-teens and teenagers.

Chapter 8

Earning the Right to Be Heard
Teaching Preteens and Teenagers

Objective

By the end of this chapter, you will decide how to earn the right to be heard by evaluating the needs of preteens and teenagers.

What on earth do they want? We look at preteens and teenagers and wonder at their abrasive behavior, their apparent disregard for authority, and the apathetic attitude that occasionally washes across their faces. We see the great effort they take to dress in bizarre colors and wear crazy clothes. Why? What on earth do they really want?

Someone Cares

Teens and preteens want to be noticed. They want to know that they are important. They want to know that someone cares. And they want to be accepted for who they are.

During the adolescent years, the search for identity is a major task. Belonging is an insatiable driving force where peer group is paramount. Through the mirror of their friends, the adolescent seeks definition and belonging. If unsuccessful in this search, teens become confused about who they are and what role they are to play in society.

With conflicting images superimposed by the media, by the schools, by the government, and by the proponents of moral relativism, there is little wonder that in quiet ways our youth are screaming out for help. We know that Jesus Christ is the answer. But how do we get them to hear us?

The Gift of Time

In youth ministry, there is no substitute for the gift of time. Spending hours at the roller skating rink, on the basketball court, at theme parks, in schools, at camps, and retreats are ways to earn the right to be heard. In turn, teens respond by showing up en masse for church events and bringing their friends with them.

A successful educational process can be *formal, nonformal,* or *informal.* The classroom setting is the traditional *formal* setting where teaching occurs with desks, chairs, blackboards or whiteboards, overheads, and computers. *Nonformal* settings are small-group meetings that usually occur in the intimacy of a living room or in the church's smaller classrooms. *Informal* education takes place anywhere, anytime, everywhere, all the time. In fact, this is how parents are instructed to teach their children God's commandments.

> These commandments that I give you today are to be upon your hearts. Impress them on your children. Talk about them when you sit at home and when you walk along the road, when you lie down and when you get up.
> —DEUTERONOMY 6:6–7

While both the formal and nonformal settings are inherently valuable processes, fleshing out the Good News—being living examples of what it means to be a Christian—is especially visible through the informal process. At a time when youth are searching for belonging and identity, "hanging out" with them and teaching informally is one of the most effective methods of teaching or discipleship. Through the informal process, leaders model the Christian lifestyle.

Jesus and the Teenager

Did Jesus spend time with teenagers? There is a hint in Scripture that young Mark may have been in the company of Jesus. Biblical history generally does not treat the Mark who wrote one of the gospels as an eyewitness to the ministry of Jesus. Rather, it is noted that he traveled with Peter, from whom he received the information that he recorded. But a closer look at the text suggests that this teenager indeed may have been an eyewitness at least to some of the major events in the life of our Lord.

On the night of his betrayal, the disciples were with Jesus in the Garden of Gethsemane. Frightened and alarmed at his arrest, they all ran. Next, we read this interesting anecdote in Mark's gospel.

> A young man, wearing nothing but a linen garment, was following Jesus. When they seized him, he fled naked, leaving his garment behind.
> —MARK 14:51

Since all of the disciples had already fled, who was there to witness this scene? It is not recorded in any other gospel, so it may be an autobiographical note of the author himself. Though too young to be a disciple, Mark probably tagged along on several occasions just to be in the company of Jesus. And at his young age, he was a faithful follower, and in fact, the last one to run—and he ran only when the soldiers tried to arrest him! Through Mark's friendship with Jesus, Peter, and the other disciples, Mark became a believer and gospel author.

———————

The first summer at my new church broke my heart. I looked around and saw dozens of teenagers faithfully attending services, some with their parents, most coming on their own. What saddened me was that besides Sunday morning, no other ministry was available for them. I remembered how vital youth ministry had been for me as a teenager.

My family life was chaotic. With a mentally ill mother, home life was unstable to say the least. I remember being sad and frightened much of the time. The unexpected was what scared me most, and I longed for the comfort and stability of routine. My father managed the best way he could. He decided that for our well-being, he needed to return home to his parents—my grandparents—and he took us children with him.

Near my grandfather's house was a small storefront church. Their youth ministry rescued my life! Every Saturday, Philip and Steven met us to rehearse for a drama ministry called "The Drama Guild." The pastor's daughter, Gladys, directed the youth choir that also rehearsed on Saturdays. How I looked forward to these weekly meetings! I found Jesus to be the faithful Friend I so desperately needed.

As I reminisced on the effect that youth ministry had on my life, I decided that I faced a wonderful opportunity to return what had so graciously been deposited into me. With a budget from the church, I rented school buses throughout the course of the summer, recruited additional adult volunteers, and took the students roller skating, swimming, and to the theme parks. Parents were responsible for paying their children's admittance fees where required, but the church sponsored those who were financially in need. Happy to have something to do with their summer days, the students invited their friends, and our small crowd slowly began to grow.

After several of these trips, I decided that it was time to have a Friday night youth meeting. The video chapel was packed with over one hundred teenagers—far more than those who had accompanied us on our outings! From this, a regular youth ministry blossomed that surprised everyone.

We loved the youth, and demonstrated it by spending precious time with them. During summer break and other major holidays, like Christmas and Easter, something exciting was planned for them to do. They knew that their youth leaders cared about them. In turn, when we planned youth services, they showed up en masse. They invited relatives, friends, and in some cases, their entire athletic team!

These students responded because of one reason, and one reason alone. By giving them the gift of time, we had earned the right to be heard.

Junior High and Middle School

In grades 6, 7, and 8, *fun* is the key word. Walk into any junior high or middle school classroom, and it's easy to see that these students have an incredible sense of humor. They love practical jokes and applaud any reason to act silly. They are capable of being serious for short spurts of time but are quick to label even the best of intentions as "boring" if it does not meet their standard of fun. They are now able to think hypothetically and understand abstract concepts, so talking and debating head the list as their preferred ways of learning.

Because they are beginning to be attracted to the opposite sex, early adolescents are very conscious of their own appearance. Part of belonging means looking like others in the peer group, so conform-

Time to Remember

Before we begin to look at each different age group and the characteristics of each group, it may be very helpful to think about your teenage years. What were your fears? What were your challenges? What was life like for you at home? How was your relationship with your siblings? Could you talk to your parents? How did you look? Did you like living inside your body? Did you have pimples? Were you popular? Were you athletic? Did you fit in with the "in" crowd? Did you have a church family? How did they meet your needs? What do you wish the church community had done differently? What questions were answered for you? What was left unanswered? Close your eyes and remember . . .

ity in dress is crucial. Not fitting in can be these students' worst nightmare. Their self-esteem hinges on external factors like hair and clothing, so leaders must help these youth identify their gifts and talents so that they feel good about something other than how they look.

Both boys and girls are on emotional roller coasters. Mood swings can be sharp and intense, quickly jumping from high to low. Though they take personal offenses quite seriously, most are willing to forgive quickly if they feel they have been treated fairly. Skill in conflict resolution is essential for those who minister to this age group.

High School

During grades 9 through 12, much of the focus is on completing high school and deciding on college and career goals. In general, high school students are intense about their music, and hero worship is at an all-time high.

High school students struggle to fit what they know of the world into what they understand about God. They are very idealistic and want the world to be fair. Accordingly, in their questions about God they often ask, "Why did God let this happen?" In addition to troubling experiences that may raise personal doubt, other students, whose religious background differs from the Christian's, challenge these students with questions about the Bible that force them to reevaluate their faith.

Understandably, where there is inconsistent behavior or hypocrisy, adolescents are quick to criticize and condemn. Parents who straddle the fence and who live different lives Monday through Saturday than they do on Sunday mornings are perhaps the biggest hindrances to their teenagers wholeheartedly owning their faith.

While they aren't looking for perfection, teenagers do demand honesty. Youth leaders who share appropriately about their struggles and successes are the ones who become "real" to their students. Effective ministry is impossible without respect, and teenagers will not respect anyone they consider to be a phony.

A Twenty-first-Century Model

Youth ministry for the twenty-first century may seem to have as its rival the Internet, e-mail, and MTV. The world is so sophisticated and moves so fast that in our churches we may ask, "How on earth can we compete?"

Be assured that computer screens are no substitute for personal contact. Relationships are what produce disciples.

Allowing teens to wrestle with their tough questions—and giving them the freedom to ask them—helps to integrate biblical truths into teenagers' everyday realities. This method demands an approach to youth ministry that is not teacher-centered but learner-centered. Rather than being passive listeners to a lecture or sermon, for example, students should be actively engaged in the learning process. In this model, the teacher is the facilitator, one who provides creative ways to help the students talk, discuss, ask questions, investigate truth, solve problems, and arrive at conclusions. Students should be digging into their Bibles, memorizing Scripture, doing research, and analyzing the issues of their day in light of the Word of God—in effect, learning in church the way they learn in school!

Preaching and teaching or lecture is necessary, but it is not the exclusive method. If leaders are not hearing what the students are thinking, if there is no way for students to interject issues they consider to be relevant into their learning environment, then ministry may not be scratching students where they itch.

Bernadette, an inquisitive teenager, attended a Filipino Baptist church. She appeared to be antagonistic because at the end of every lesson she would ask, "So what's the point?" After lecturing so diligently, the teacher felt frustration that made him feel like pulling out his hair.

The assistant teacher, Diosdado Portugal, was a Christian education major. From what he had learned in class, he began to analyze the difficulties they were experiencing on Sundays with Bernadette. He explained to the head teacher that Bernadette was not learning simply by listening. Somehow she and the other students needed a chance to see how these lessons fit into their lives.

The lead teacher began to invite the students to share what was going on in their lives, and student participation increased dramatically. As the teens asked more questions, they became more interested in what the Bible had to say. As a result, the students experienced a relevant teaching-learning time, and the teachers left feeling fulfilled.

"Bernadette's honesty forced us to change our teaching style," said the assistant teacher. "Our lessons had to become more interactive."

Leader's Tip

Before students go on any trips, parents must sign permission slips that give the volunteers permission to take their children off the church's campus. Permission slips also provide information about students' allergies or illnesses. Parents are responsible for reviewing the church's rules with their child and must sign that they have done so. (See appendix B for a sample "Travel Permission Slip" that may provide the basis for developing your own.)

Training

Interactive, another way to earn the right to be heard, characterizes what should happen in every youth ministry. Leaders and teachers need to practice the art of listening to their students. And youth leaders must be trained. Period.

B.O.S.S. and Youth for Christ

Al and Hattie Hollingsworth, a dynamite Christian couple with a multifaceted ministry located in Southern California, have developed an intensive program that is one of the best for training youth workers and student leaders. Based on solid biblical principles, "Building On Spiritual Substance" (B.O.S.S.) emphasizes a Christian lifestyle of leadership, discipline, accountability, and responsibility. Once they have successfully completed the training, youth leaders can be certified to replicate the B.O.S.S. training in their individual churches.[1]

In addition to providing training, Youth for Christ, a national parachurch ministry that evangelizes high school campuses, offers ministry events throughout the year. They do the planning. You just bring the kids. Events like YFC's *OVERTIME* is one example. Students stay up all night, which is why it's called overtime. They go to amusement parks, concerts, skating rinks, and the like, from one activity to another. At a designated point in the evening (or early morning!), students sit still long enough to hear a power-packed gospel message that challenges them to make decisions for Christ. *OVERTIME* and events like this are creative ways to blend fun with ministry.

---

[1]For more information about the B.O.S.S. program, call (909) 861-3846.

Hispanic Internship

We can all agree that some of the best training occurs in hands-on ministry. Internship programs provide just that by allowing leaders the opportunity to learn from the experts through on-the-job training. One of the best this country has to offer is KIDWORKS, a ministry for children and teens sponsored by the Hispanic Ministry Center directed by Larry Acosta.[2]

Interns actually live in the neighborhoods where the ministry takes place, conducting KidsClub, a program for elementary children, and forming mentoring groups to teach a Christian value-based curriculum. For youth ministry, the interns work alongside other youth leaders to run handball tournaments, start or assist with Bible studies, and spend time with teens to show them that they are loved and valued. It's a missions experience that's guaranteed to change a life, and the local church will benefit once the youth leaders return home.

This is just a sampling of the training that is available. Various denominations and other parachurch ministries also train youth workers in local, regional, and national conferences. Providing budgets for these leaders to become better equipped is well worth the expense. For those who attend, learning about new ministry models, networking, and sharing ideas are major benefits. If one desires to pursue children's or youth ministry full-time, completing specialized courses of study at a Christian college, university, or seminary increases expertise and maximizes marketability.

Involving Parents

The teenage years are as challenging for parents as they are for the students. Often problems can be avoided if parents know what to expect and are taught how to respond. Leaders must be intentional about involving parents during these important years because, ideally, the church should reinforce what's being taught in the home. Developing communication skills, abstinence education, and college preparation are a few examples of seminar topics that equip both parents and their teens.

As much as we attempt to involve parents in their child's Christian education, it's a fallacy to always assume that what is being taught in the classroom is reinforced at home. Below is an example from a junior high youth worker that demonstrates that parents may some-

---

[2]For more information about KIDWORKS, contact codirectors David Benavides and John Lewis by calling (714) 554-7500.

times misunderstand doctrine. Therefore, it may be the teacher's responsibility to effectively communicate biblical truths to the students. Volunteer teacher La Roya Jordan explains:

I was teaching about salvation according to Romans 10:9. We had studied this passage for several weeks, and I stressed that when we accept Jesus Christ as Savior, he changes us and makes us brand-new.

One Sunday after class, a student asked to speak to me. He was obviously upset and very worried. I asked him what was wrong.

"My father told me that I could never be saved," he said. Apparently, this student was a major problem in school, and his father, who was faithful in bringing his son to class, had decided that salvation was only for those who *deserved* to be saved. He had told his son repeatedly that there was no hope for him.

I sat this young man down and we looked at Romans 10:9 together. "What is God saying? Read the verse out loud."

"That if you confess with your mouth, 'Jesus is Lord,' and believe in your heart that God raised him from the dead, you will be saved," he read.

"Who does *you* include?" I asked. I helped him to see that "you" meant *him*. I told him that I was sorry that his father didn't understand how much God loves and accepts everyone who trusts in him. That morning he prayed in earnest to receive Christ as his Lord and Savior. I will never forget that moment.

Teach the Basics

When we teach, it is probably best to assume initially that students know very little about the Christian faith, including salvation. This is especially important in our contemporary culture. Many adults have decided not to "force" their children to go to church; therefore, some teenagers and young adults have grown up without the benefit of a rich Christian heritage.

In many instances we are teaching a generation of unchurched young people. We cannot assume that they know the account of Noah's ark, Moses at the Red Sea, or any passage familiar to those who grew up in Sunday school. We must teach and explain these passages as if students are learning this information for the first time, because in many instances they are.

———

Once a year we used to take our junior high and high school students on a winter retreat. This trip was such a favorite among our kids that parents used this opportunity to ground their children if they had not performed up to standard during the first half of the school year. Desperate, students called for help. In turn, I telephoned their parents and begged them to please make this the exception.

"Now is not the time to ground your child! If you let her attend, she will come back different," would be my pleading promise. Parents trusted me and obliged. Now with the youth obligated to be on their best behavior, we departed.

The camp we attended guaranteed life-changing ministry and endless fun. Maurice Miller, a veteran youth worker, was a genius at planning the most unique activities and events. By the end of the Thursday-through-Saturday retreat, dozens of young people would give their lives to Christ. Counselors, exhausted from the packed three-day routine, would be overwhelmed with the fruit of their prayers and labor. It was truly an amazing experience.

One year, we had an exceptionally large number of students that we piled into buses for the drive to the mountains. And, as usual, there were several other churches that came with their students, too.

After the first session, the adults knew that something was different, and it was not good. We met together and prayed, and the Holy Spirit revealed the problem to us. Too many students were unsaved, and it was nearly impossible to minister. So rather than waiting to give the invitation for salvation on the final night, we decided to give the invitation at the beginning of the retreat.

What a difference! It was like a breath of fresh air—the breath of the Holy Spirit! Attitudes changed. Although students continued to make decisions throughout the course of the next few days, starting with salvation was the place for that year's ministry to begin.

———

Sex, Drugs, Drinking, and Suicide

Students who have a poor self-image or who come from a dysfunctional family may end up flirting with sex, drugs, drinking, dropping out, and joining gangs—or any destructive combination thereof. Of course, most teens, even those from the best of homes, struggle with these issues, too. Peer pressure is strong enough to push a student beyond the boundaries of safety, reason, and simple common sense.

Youth leaders should have resources at their fingertips for Christian and social service agencies that specialize in providing emergency help for teens in trouble. A local teen suicide hotline number should be visibly posted in the youth office for quick and easy reference. By law, all threats of suicide must be reported to authorities immediately. Don't try to judge the severity of the threat. Leave this decision to the professionals.

Abstinence Education

In the age of HIV and AIDS, teaching abstinence should be a major component of every Christian education ministry. Studies have shown that students who attend church one or more times a week are less likely to become sexually active. This is wonderful news, but church attendance alone is not enough. We need to do more, and we can.

Sex is discussed everywhere except in the church. But it is here that the standard should be raised and the issue addressed. Abstinence begins with obedience to God's Word. The biblical basis for a positive approach to abstinence education is that God created sex, that it is good because he created it, and that it is best enjoyed within the boundaries of a loving marriage relationship.

Leader's Tip

When There's Suicide

Make sure that all youth workers are aware of your church policy for reporting suicide threats or attempts. Flesh out details with the counseling ministry, or call the teen suicide hotline for practical what-to-do steps. Review the policy periodically in staff meetings. The safest policy is to report any suicide threat to the authorities immediately.

When There's Sexual or Physical Abuse

Any suspicion of sexual or physical abuse must be reported. Respecting confidentiality does not extend to cases where minors are in danger. Call the police or social services to find out your state's policy for reporting such offenses.

While most high school sex education classes teach students how to have "safer sex," abstinence education teaches the importance of making healthy decisions that are essential to every aspect of life, not merely the delay of sexual intercourse until marriage. Christian chastity programs where teens make vows of abstinence are excellent ways to capitalize on positive peer pressure. Accountability is created when students make commitments in the presence of their friends. It's a powerful visual . . . a memorable moment.

Equipping students who attend public schools as "peer models" who are articulate in classroom debates or in discussions around the lunchroom table is another way that Christian education can meet the needs of teenagers. Peer models can also be trained to teach resistance skills—how to say "No"—to their friends and classmates. Those who successfully complete such training and who remain abstinent might be given special awards such as scholarships to college by their local church or denomination. Abstinence is experiencing a revival around the country! What better group for it to influence than the youth in the local church.

Rites of Passage

In African-American churches, a Rites of Passage, or a manhood training for boys, is an excellent way to build Christian character in young men. This tradition dates back to the motherland where boys were removed from the village by the adult males. Away from daily comforts, they were taught skills that prepared them to assume responsibility in their community. They returned home as men.

In churches, Rites of Passage ministries teach young males self-respect, respect for other people and their property, and responsibility and accountability to themselves, their families, their community, and their church. Spiritually mature men who have been discipled and trained act as mentors and role models. Teaching occurs in formal classes and through informal activities such as sports events, mission trips, visits to museums, plays, and concerts.

This is a valuable ministry for all boys ages 11 to 14. My husband instituted a year-long Rites of Passage at our church. The boys meet on Saturday mornings and spend most of the day with their leaders who are called *champions*. The success of this program has caught the attention of the entire city, including our mayor! Not only have the boys been influenced positively, but the champions have, too.

Responding to a challenge at a retreat to become involved in ministry, Reggie Varra joined Rites of Passage and committed to serve as a champion for one year. He completed his training and was diligent in meeting his responsibilities as a mentor.

After several months, Reggie was offered a major promotion at his job where he worked as group plant manager of a large manufacturing plant. This opportunity meant that he would be responsible for coordinating the start-up of a new 500,000-square-foot facility. The salary increase was huge—a career dream come true.

Reggie, however, had one major problem. This promotion demanded that he relocate three thousand miles away to New York. Rather than disappoint his Rites of Passage students, he turned down the offer. What seemed like a major sacrifice to others (certainly, God would understand!) was not even a second thought to Reggie. He was sowing into the lives of these boys, and leaving with the task undone—no matter how justifiable—was not even an option.

Months after refusing this promotion, Reggie was offered another, but this time it did not require relocating. And the salary increase was even more than the one previously offered! By determining to honor his commitment, Reggie experienced the truth that God honors those who honor him.

Not Against Flesh

For young men without the benefit of such programs, gangs often become their existence. From New York to California we lament over all of the young people who are buried too soon due to inner city gang warfare. So effective ministry to youth must include teaching them the reality of spiritual warfare, and that they can win this war with the Lord's help. Drama is a tool that educates as well as entertains. Here is an anecdote about a play entitled "Not Against Flesh."

One summer we buried three teenagers. Two died as a result of gang violence. One died accidentally. He was a good student, a star athlete, but he carried a gun to protect himself from the bullies who threatened him because they considered him to be a nerd. Since he was smart, he was a target.

One night, on the way back from a game, he played an unwise game of Russian roulette and lost. As he was pulling the trigger with the gun at his temple, his friends laughed and egged him on. They had no idea that the gun was actually loaded.

Why are they killing themselves? How can we help our teenagers see that the Devil is the one encouraging them to pull that trigger? Through prayers of intercession, and inspired by Frank Peretti's book, *This Present Darkness,* the play "Not Against Flesh" was birthed.

It began like this. After several weeks of prayer, I woke up one morning with the idea for a play based on this passage: "For our struggle is not against flesh and blood, but against the rulers, against the authorities, against the powers of this dark world and against the spiritual forces of evil in the heavenly realms" (Eph. 6:12).

The plot was rather elementary. There were two gangs—a female gang and a male gang. One of the girls in the female gang becomes pregnant and has to decide what to do. One of the male gang members tries to get out of his gang and is murdered in the process. Throughout the play, angels intervene, speaking to the youth and inspiring them to make the right choice. Coaxing, taunting, and prompting the youth to destruction are the demons. The angels, of course, wore beautiful white costumes. The demons were dressed hideously in frightening masks and dark garments. Without acknowledging their presence, the actors responded to the advice of these spirits, and their decisions propelled the plot to its climax.

The play ends with the funeral of the lead character. In the church, when the sermon is preached, the gang members accept Christ.

To get this play into script format, I asked a friend to draft a treatment, a fuller version of my notes from which a script could be written. We had no idea whether people would be interested in such a production, so we decided to give an open call for auditions.

Although we specified teenagers, the aspiring actors in our audience included adults as well and a few people who could sing. Fortunately, we had more than enough for a cast, but one tiny detail was still missing . . . the actual script!

God, the Master of what I call "Holy Hook-Ups," sent twin writers Lester Griffin and Levaniel Griffin, who also had a burden to rescue our youth. They were thrilled to take the treatment and develop dialog for the play from it. We grouped the actors first—teenage girls and boys would be our gang members, and the adults would portray angels and demons. We began rehearsals immediately.

The term "hot off the press" was probably designed for us. Each Saturday, the script would arrive fresh from the computer, and we would go to work. We began each rehearsal with a fifteen-minute devotional that taught a truth portrayed in the play. "Actors" learned about spiritual warfare and about their authority in Jesus Christ. Then we covered ourselves in prayer and rehearsed.

At the end of four weeks, we were as ready as amateurs could be. We had stagehands who worked behind the scenes with the set (actually husbands and wives were recruited to help). A clothing designer and children's church teacher fashioned the costumes for the angels and found the eeriest masks for the demons! We printed up flyers, prayed, and gave them to the cast and crew to distribute. The play was scheduled a week from that date on the following Friday night.

We were not prepared for the response. Our church auditorium, which at that time held about 450 people, was beyond capacity with over 700 teenagers! We tried to fit everyone in and placed folding chairs up and down the aisles. We sat teens on the floor, practically to the edge of the stage.

Our church's expert sound and light technician worked miracles with our tiny budget. Excited because their friends were in the audience, the actors were outstanding. During the final scene, the preacher, who happened to be a real one, stepped off of the stage and extended the invitation to the audience just as we had rehearsed.

Teenagers poured from the pews. When the preacher said, "Don't let any demon hold you in your seat," the floodgates opened again and the altar filled so that there was no standing room left in the aisles. That night, over 400 teenagers accepted Jesus Christ. It was truly awesome!

Powerful Ministry

"Not Against Flesh" ran again a month later, also to a similar crowd. If there is an area of ministry that is powerful to change lives, it is drama.

Skits and plays are a creative, effective means for delivering God's truth. They also provide the opportunity to teach content that is relevant to the learner. Creative methods keep our ministries fresh and timely. Never should we conduct youth ministry the same way that it was done years ago.

In our church, the youth minister has implemented a new winning idea—training leaders who head Christian sororities and fraternities. Rather than resembling those typically found on the college campus, these sororities and fraternities are Bible-centered and spiritual, challenging the youth to evaluate the music to which they listen and to adopt godly habits in their daily lives. It's working! What an example of keeping in step with the times.

Never, Never, Never Give Up!

In youth ministry, it's easy to give up on our students. Every teacher knows the dread of entering the classroom week after week and facing that one *special* teenager. We tell ourselves quietly in our hearts that this child will never amount to anything worthwhile. We are convinced that he will never absorb our teaching because he never sits still and isn't quiet long enough to listen.

Time and experience teach one valuable lesson: Never, never, never give up!

I used to throw Travon out of my junior high classroom every week. He was not a bad kid; he was just mischievous. Travon always had the class laughing at his pranks and jokes and before long, he managed to get on my last two nerves. I usually asked Travon to leave within 10 minutes of arriving in class.

In spite of his behavior, Travon knew his Bible. He had grown up in our children's ministry, and he had been taught at home from the time he was a child. If he could keep still long enough for the review portion of the lesson, other students learned from him. Travon always knew the answers to questions, and he was excellent with Scripture memorization. And, oh, how he could pray!

But when he wasn't talking, he was laughing, and so were the other students. With him in the room, teaching seemed like a waste of time. In our teachers' meetings, when we named the child who challenged us most, usually his name surfaced. Needless to say, no one expected him to do anything serious for the Lord.

We were wrong. Today, Travon is one of the most dynamic young men in our ministry. Midway through his college education, he plans to attend seminary to become a minister.

Recently, Travon preached a short sermon at our annual Christmas dinner for teachers, and he brought tears to our eyes. Our pastor, who also attended the celebration, invited Travon to preach at one of the Sunday morning services. As you can imagine, the auditorium was filled with ... teachers.

Travon is one of our biggest success stories. He teaches the junior high class and regularly ministers to our students. Committed to godliness and personal purity, Travon is a testimony to the truth that no matter how frustrated we become, we should never, never, never give up!

Do You Remember?

In this chapter we evaluated the importance of earning the right to be heard as we minister to preteens and teenagers. Here is a summary of major points to remember.

- *The Gift of Time.* The key to youth ministry is giving the gift of time. Educational settings can be formal (classroom), nonformal (small group), or informal (learning through relationship). The informal process provides a living example by modeling what it means to be a Christian.
- *Junior High and Middle School.* The key word is "fun." Youth reject anything that they label as "boring." They struggle with peer pressure and have intense needs to belong. Capable of hypothetical thinking and understanding abstract concepts, they love talking and debating. They are conscious of their appearance and are beginning to be attracted to the opposite sex.
- *High School.* Intense about their music, high school students are prone to hero worship. They are idealistic and have questions about God and their faith. Critical of hypocrites or those who behave inconsistently with what they profess, teens demand honesty before giving their respect.
- *Twenty-first-Century Ministry Model.* The high-tech influence of our modern day is no competition for relationships that result from youth leaders who spend time with kids. In the classroom, effective teaching encourages student discussion and interaction.
- *Training.* Training is key to an effective youth leader. Parachurch agencies and denominations offer seminars that provide ministry models and networking opportunities.

Youth workers considering full-time ministry might consider attending Christian colleges and seminaries.

- *Involve Parents.* Successful youth ministry involves and trains the parents. Ideally, the church should reinforce the Christian values that are being taught in the home, but we cannot assume that all youth have this foundation.
- *Teach the Basics.* Don't assume that youth are familiar with the basics, such as salvation. Always begin here.
- *Sex, Drugs, Drinking, and Suicide.* Have policies established beforehand to deal with these emergencies. Call the local suicide hotline to report all suicide threats, and notify the police and social services of all cases involving physical or sexual abuse.
- *Abstinence Education.* Studies show that children who attend church one or more times a week are less likely to become sexually active. The church should be proactive in teaching abstinence education.
- *Rites of Passage, Drama, Fraternities, and Sororities.* Creative methods keep our youth ministries fresh and timely. Never should we conduct youth ministry the same way that it was done years ago. Don't be afraid to try something new.
- *Never, Never, Never Give Up!* No matter how hopeless kids may seem, *never* give up on them!

Another Challenge

If youth ministry is no easy task, teaching adults also has its challenges. The key is to capitalize on teachable moments. That's what we will discuss next.

Chapter 9

Teachable Moments
Teaching Adults

Objective

By the end of this chapter, you will judge the merits of capitalizing on teachable moments by evaluating how adults are motivated to learn.

The best time to teach adults is when they are most ready to learn. Special events like baptism, marriage, and childbirth are times when new information is sincerely welcomed and much appreciated. Meeting adults at life's important intersections capitalizes on what educators call *teachable moments*.

Voluntary Learners

Adults are voluntary learners. Wise parents may insist that their children attend the children's and youth services, but after high school the decision to go to a Bible study is usually left up to the individual.

With the time constraints of day-to-day living, adults balance their church attendance among work, family, friends, and recreation. Unless they are spiritually mature, most adults will only enter the learning environment—the Bible study or classroom—when they have a need. If gaining new information will help them to fulfill personal or family goals, then adults are ready to learn.

Readiness to learn is key to teachable moments. Learning is most effective when adults have a need for the information. The teacher can help *motivate* students to learn, but the teacher cannot *make* students learn. Of course, the Master Teacher was a master of teachable moments.

The Everyday and Ordinary

Jesus capitalized on teachable moments in the everyday, ordinary experiences of his learners to meet them at their point of need. As with the woman at the well, Jesus often taught deep truths through common events.

She needed water. There was Jesus, waiting at the well. His was the water she really needed to quench her parched soul.

> Jesus answered, "Everyone who drinks this water will be thirsty again, but whoever drinks the water I give him will never thirst. Indeed, the water I give him will become in him a spring of water welling up to eternal life."
> The woman said to him, "Sir, give me this water so that I won't get thirsty and have to keep coming here to draw water."
>
> —JOHN 4:13–15

In the ordinary business of her everyday task, this woman found eternal life. Teachable moments occur in the everyday, ordinary lives of our adult learners, too. In addition to offering traditional Bible studies, our responsibility is to shape curriculum that addresses their life needs and experiences.

What are some of those needs?

College-aged Students

As students complete high school, they face many challenges. Going to college, finding the right job or career, and beginning to live independently from their parents are major tasks for the college-aged student. The church can help them choose options that set a solid foundation for their lives.

With those who decide to continue their education, Christian education can play an important role. Offering courses to help students pass required tests, providing scholarships, and helping students complete applications are a few ways that the church can prove itself valuable in the lives of the young people it serves.

Teaching young adults how to pray in the process, how to depend on God, and how to memorize Scripture that encourages them during stressful times are ways to integrate biblical principles. Modeling godliness gives them an example to follow as they begin to make more decisions on their own. Once in college, keeping in contact with students by sending them letters and sermon tapes helps to maintain their connection with the local church body.

But what about those young adults who have given up and dropped out? Sidetracked by their inability to cope with the pressures of family problems or school, and suffering from lack of motivation and low self-esteem, some may need alcohol or drug rehabilitation. The church can redirect them. Specialized classes based on the forgiving, redemptive love of Jesus Christ will help young people get back on track.

Computer training is another service that Christian education can provide to help young adults. Setting up a computer lab is a timely ministry for the church that desires to serve its community as well. And think of it! Computers will give nonmembers a reason to step inside the church building!

Postcollege-aged Adults

From ages 22 to 35, postcollege-aged adults have the tasks of choosing careers, finding jobs, and establishing meaningful relationships. Christian education can respond to these needs by providing career counseling and assistance with job placement. To help with interpersonal relationships, we can offer classes that teach the biblical view of dating and marriage. Teaching adults how to develop long-term interpersonal relationships centers on helping them understand who they are in Christ and knowing that God has a purpose for their lives. What an excellent opportunity to impart spiritual truths!

Singles' Bible studies, retreats, and events where singles can meet one another address their needs in practical ways. If Christians are to marry Christians (and they are!), then the church is the place for Christian singles to meet other Christian singles. Bible studies that do not provide a time during class for people to talk with one another are missing a great opportunity. Imagine! Singles may meet their mate in a neighbor nudge or small-group discussion.

The needs of single parents can also be met in their teachable moments. They may need help in finding affordable child care while they work, and some services can be offered right in the church. To help move mothers from welfare to work, for example, government subsidies have been designated specifically for churches to develop day care facilities. Your local social service office is the place to begin to learn how to tap into these resources.

Parenting classes, premarital counseling, ministry for couples, and financial planning are additional ways to meet adults in their everyday, ordinary tasks. Infusing scriptural principles into these vital areas gives men and women a biblical framework that helps them develop a Christian worldview.

Middle-aged Adults

From 35 to 55, adults are beginning to focus their attention on the world around them to leave a legacy for the following generation. Most have completed their educational pursuits and want to deepen their relationship with Jesus Christ.

Because middle-aged adults have the personal freedom and financial resources to travel, many have a growing interest in missions. Short-term trips and "vacations" that encourage interaction with various cultures are wise ways to spread the Gospel. And pairing these adults with teenagers accomplishes two goals simultaneously.

Pairing works in other areas, too. Matching married couples with newlyweds in a marriage mentoring ministry is another opportunity for Christian education. Actually, this ministry might be an extension of the counseling ministry, but it is an idea worth exploring no matter under which umbrella it falls.

Leader's Tip

When was the last time that you reviewed your church's mission statement? Periodic reviews will help keep you in step with your pastor's vision. As you evaluate your church's purpose, think about the adult ministries currently in place. What's right? What's wrong? What's missing? If there could be an ideal, what would it look like at your church? What is preventing this from happening?

To begin, talk with your church leadership. As the ministry moves to accomplish its goal, what are the next steps? What will the adults in your church need to know in order to get there? For example, do you need evangelism training? Does the church need to offer a class to help people discover their spiritual gifts to equip them for ministry in the church? Are small groups needed to build relationships? Does there need to be accountability in discipleship so that people can learn how to live the Christian life?

Talk to the men and women in the congregation. What are their needs? What would they like to learn? How can the church better serve them? And how can they better serve the church?

As you evaluate your congregation, where do you think the adults are spiritually? Are they babes in Christ, in need of a stronger biblical foundation? What do you wish they knew about the Bible, but don't? Now, pray. God *will* give you direction for your ministry.

While some who are married are seeking new and exciting vistas, others may be recovering from divorce or the premature death of a spouse. Again, the church can meet their needs. Small groups that focus on these specific issues guide people through these traumatic experiences to provide fellowship, hope, and healing.

Not to be forgotten are those who are caring for sick and aging parents. They might appreciate the support and camaraderie of others who have similar responsibilities. In addition to helping one another with information or referrals, these adults can pray together for strength and wisdom as they walk through life's transition when the child becomes the parent.

Late Adulthood

People in the years 55 and over may have some of the challenges of the earlier years such as redefining career or family, but at this age, needs shift as late adults begin to transition out of the workforce. Adjusting to physical changes, preparing for retirement, and helping with or caring for grandchildren are major tasks of late adulthood.

Although spiritual maturity is not to be assumed merely because one has aged, some of these adults may be able to teach, counsel, and minister. Late adults feel valued when active and working in kingdom building.

Keep the Vision

It's obvious that few individual churches can develop every Christian education ministry idea that has been suggested for adults. And some of these ideas, such as support groups, may be the responsibility of the counseling or discipleship ministry. When deciding how to design classes, remember that Christian education ministries should flow from the senior pastor's vision.

Bible Study

While we seek to creatively develop classes, traditional Bible study still has a necessary place in Christian education. The curriculum should be chosen to meet the congregation's needs. Weekly Bible classes, including a class at noon for those who are retired, who work evenings, or who want to study the Bible during their lunch hour, are a must in every ministry.

New Members Class

If adults want to become members of a local church or become involved in its ministries, here is an excellent teachable moment. Offering New Members classes, which must be completed in order to become a member, is the opportune way to capitalize on their readiness to learn.

To integrate new believers into the church body, the curriculum should teach basic doctrine along with the church's philosophy of ministry. Upon completion of a series (whether 4, 8, 10, or 12 weeks, depending on the church), certificates of membership can be awarded. Those who miss one or two weeks of classes can make them up in the next class cycle.

Remember that people work, travel, and in general, maintain hectic lifestyles, so schedule classes to allow for some flexibility. Here's a suggestion. Offer week #1 of your curriculum on Sunday morning (prior to or following a service) and teach the same lesson on one or two weeknights. Then teach the next lesson beginning with Sunday of week #2, and repeat this lesson on the weeknights. Such scheduling provides options for students and enables them to adjust their day planners when necessary so that no matter what comes up, they can attend one class per week.

Upon completion, members may be allowed to participate in ministries such as the choir or usher board, or to volunteer in children's church. More importantly, the teachable moment has been maximized! New members understand what they believe and are now on a solid foundation and in step with the rest of the congregation.

It has been said that when people belong to a church but are inactive for a year, they are less likely to become active and join a ministry after that. Perhaps this is why most churches have the 20–100 ratio: 20 percent of the people do 100 percent of the work! *Discover Your Purpose*—a class designed to help believers identify their spiritual gifts and match these with the ministries in their church—might ideally follow a new members class.

Seminars and Workshops

Workshops and seminars are additional ways to intersect the everyday, ordinary lives of our adult learners. Old and New Testament "Walk Thru the Bible" seminars give people a good overview of the Bible and get them excited about studying God's Word.[1]

---

[1] For more information on Walk Thru the Bible Ministries, call (770) 458-9300.

Seminars on praise and worship explain how to communicate with God and appropriate his power in our lives. Prayer seminars teach people how to pray according to Scripture so that their faith is developed and strengthened. Offering these periodically to the entire church body without specifying an age group allows anyone who is motivated to participate.

Disequilibrium

Remember that in a teachable moment, people are ready to learn. Implied in this is urgency! Learners want to solve a problem, relieve pain or discomfort, or answer questions that may have them feeling unsettled. In educational circles this tension or disturbance is called *disequilibrium*. It happens when learners feel that their reality is disturbed or their world seems a little off balance.

Learners sometimes experience disequilibrium when they encounter the unexpected. When life does not fit into neat categories, when events occur out of sync, when patterns are disturbed, there is disequilibrium. Often God designs these moments precisely with the intention of teaching us. And since we want to return to our previous calm state, we are eager and ready to learn. He definitely has our attention.

Nicodemus experienced such a moment. Because Jesus was so unpopular among the Pharisees, Nicodemus decided to talk to Jesus when no one else was around. The cloak of night presented that perfect opportunity.

Apparently, his earlier encounters with Jesus left Nicodemus feeling quite curious. Something was left unanswered. He had to know more. Jesus did not tiptoe around this tension in Nicodemus. In fact, he created more tension to maximize the lesson his new student was about to learn.

In the process of showering compliments on Jesus, Nicodemus was unprepared when he was told that he could not even see the kingdom of God unless he was born again. Puzzled and tense, Nicodemus struggled to correlate this new information with what he already knew about being born again.

> "How can a man be born when he is old?" Nicodemus asked. "Surely he cannot enter a second time into his mother's womb to be born!"
> —John 3:4

His disequilibrium is apparent. Although being born again was a familiar concept to the Jews, Nicodemus could not fathom how this could apply to him at his stage of life. He did not ask, "How can a man be born again?" but "How can a man be born *when he is old?*"

In Pharisaic Judaism, there were six different ways of being born again. When Gentiles converted to Judaism, they were said to be "born again." When a man was crowned king, he was said to be "born again." Nicodemus did not qualify for either of these two categories, but he did qualify for the remaining four.

When a Jewish boy becomes bar mitzvah at the age of 13, he is said to be "born again," so Nicodemus was born again the first time while a teenager. When a Jewish man married, he was said to be "born again." One of the rules for a member of the Sanhedrin was that he must be married, and Nicodemus was a member of the Sanhedrin, so he was "born again" the second time when he married. When a Jew was ordained as a rabbi, he was "born again." Since Nicodemus was a Pharisee, he had been ordained as a rabbi and thus had been "born again" the third time. Nicodemus was "born again" the fourth time when he became the head of a rabbinical school. The term "a teacher of Israel" is the title for the head of a rabbinical school (John 3:10).[2]

Nicodemus had experienced all of the rebirths possible to him as a Jew. He had done everything right, but now he was being told that something else was lacking in his life. What disequilibrium!

Here is a perfect example of how the Master Teacher shook his student's reality to introduce him to spiritual birth. That Nicodemus came to faith in Christ as Messiah is evident in the events following the Crucifixion, when Joseph of Arimathea came for Jesus' body.

> He was accompanied by Nicodemus, the man who earlier had visited Jesus at night. Nicodemus brought a mixture of myrrh and aloes, about seventy-five pounds.
>
> —JOHN 19:39

Teachers must not fear or avoid tension. We must identify teachable moments and wisely navigate our students through the state of disequilibrium to connect them with God's truth.

As pastor of Christian education, one of the ministries I inherited was coordinating and organizing baby dedications. In the African-American church, the birth of a child is an event celebrated by the entire family who, whether saved or unsaved, flocks to

---

[2]Arnold G. Fruchtenbaum, *Nicodemus, A Rabbi's Quest* (Tustin, CA: Ariel Ministries, 1983).

churches that offer this ministry. On the Sundays when babies are dedicated, mothers, fathers, godparents, grandparents, aunts, uncles, nieces, nephews, and cousins gather to participate in this ceremony.

How can this traditional ceremony be transformed into a teachable moment? I wondered. I prayed and asked for guidance and direction. The Holy Spirit gave clear answers through the questions that circled in my own mind.

Why do parents dedicate their children? Are both of the parents saved? Are the godparents saved? If not, why are they giving their children back to God if they do not first know him themselves? Why go through all of this effort if they don't know why they are doing what they are doing?

The answer, of course, is tradition. Most families are ignorant of the biblical precedent behind baby dedication as found in I Samuel 1:27–28. But they have learned that when a child is born, this is the thing to do.

In the process of my questioning, God lent me one of his creative ideas. Why not offer a class as a prerequisite for all parents and godparents who want to dedicate their babies in our church? The curriculum flowed straight from the heart of God, I believe, and it had one goal—to find out whether or not parents and godparents are saved according to Romans 10:9–10.

In the very first class, only one family attended—a grandmother with her daughter, a single parent. I had never seen this daughter before, and I sensed that the grandmother was grateful for any opportunity to get her child to come to church. After talking about the baby, we then focused on the curriculum that was now in the form of a booklet. Because the questions were already in print, this young mother could not take any of the points personally.

I read the questions and asked her about her relationship with God. She swallowed her surprise, but I could almost hear, "But I thought we were here to talk about babies!" I answered her unasked question by saying, "God orchestrated your baby's birth just so that you could be in this class today and hear about the wonderful plan he has for your life."

By the end of the class, she had prayed to accept Jesus Christ as her Savior. How amazing! A convert in the baby dedication class!

Afterward I went to my office to rejoice, but instead my face was washed in tears. I thought about the hundreds of families who had stood in front of churches dedicating their children. I thought about the many unsaved husbands whose lives might have been changed had we maximized this teachable moment. From then on,

I was determined never to let slip this requirement for mothers and fathers, godmothers and godfathers.

An average of 20 to 30 people now attend class each month. Before we meet, there is always a call or two from parents or godparents asking to be excused from attending the class, but we stress that attendance is mandatory. We believe that we must do all that we can to help people meet Jesus. And usually in every class, someone accepts him as Savior.

Baby Dedication Class

Attendance in the baby dedication class is mandatory for parents who want their baby to be dedicated. Because they play such a vital role in the lives of the children, godparents must also attend. If there is a legitimate excuse, like an inflexible work schedule, the teacher may meet with this parent individually. If godparents are traveling from out of town, they may attend a same-day session prior to the ceremony.

However, attendance at the general session is encouraged because the entire class participates in winning the lost to Christ. Men usually are invited to give their testimonies if the unsaved person is male. While unsaved husbands might resist coming to church, they will usually attend a two-hour class because they want the baby to be dedicated.

A pastor or an elder teaches the class. This is important because of the mildly confrontational nature of the curriculum. A person who is in authority and who is respected has "permission" to confront.

Each attendee wears a name tag so that the teacher can address individuals personally. Parents complete the paperwork for the certificates first, and the teacher or an assistant reviews them to make certain all information is written clearly.

Next, we pray and then the class begins. By way of introduction, parents and godparents share their names, relationship to the baby, whether or not they have accepted Jesus Christ as personal Savior, and a Scripture that reassures them of salvation. This hook sets the night's agenda and gives the teacher a pretty good idea of those individuals who need salvation. Completing new members, attending weekly Bible study, spending personal time with God in prayer, and living godly lives are additional decisions that parents and godparents are encouraged to make.

By using this approach, the monthly baby dedication ceremony takes on new meaning, as the following letter indicates. It deepens the commitment of the family to raise this child in a godly home. Also, the entire congregation prays with and for the entire family and promises to model godliness before these little ones. (See appendix B for sample materials relating to Baby Dedication.)

October 7, 1997

Dear Dr. Tolbert,

To God be the glory for the great things He has done! I could not let the opportunity pass for me to express my sincere appreciation to you for your assistance. Your insight and eagerness to reach families as they dedicate their children unto the Lord is extraordinary.

God is using you in a mighty way to educate others on how to develop an effective Baby Dedication ministry. And it will have a long-term benefit to the child, as well as to the parents, godparents, grandparents, and the entire family.

The material you so graciously shared with us has been a valuable tool in reaching the hearts of many. Through this I have experienced Baby Dedication classes as another way to share the Gospel of Jesus Christ. It has provided me the opportunity to educate parents about the seriousness of the Baby Dedication ceremony, to instill godly principles, and to enlighten them on their responsibility as parents.

We have been using the material you introduced for several months. I must say, I was truly excited as I watched the Holy Spirit move in each session. As a result, the Prosperity Family has witnessed three people accept Christ as their Personal Savior. Five people rededicated their lives, and two people became members. Praise God for all that He has done and is going to do through the Baby Dedication classes.

In His Love,

Ray Rodgers, Senior Pastor
Prosperity Baptist Church

Baptism

Baptism is another teachable moment. Repeating the *purpose* of baptism (obedience), the *prerequisite* for baptism (salvation), the *picture* of baptism (the death, burial, and resurrection of Jesus Christ), and the *public confession* of baptism (before family and friends) helps new believers understand what they are about to do.

The goal of the baptism class is to exhort believers to live holy. They are taught that since baptism identifies them with the universal church as well as with the local church body, we have a responsibility to Christians everywhere to live obedient lives. "Don't bring shame to the family name!"

In this class, believers are also taught about the ordinance of Communion. Here they learn why we take Communion and what partaking of the bread and wine represent.

Class is held the week preceding baptism and lasts one hour. Holding the class several days in advance allows for pastoral follow-up should any significant questions arise from anyone who is to be baptized. It also gives ample time for the certificates to be completed.

There is a sacred place for ceremony, and baptism is one of those ceremonies to be treasured. It presents a most beautiful picture of identifying with Christ. Children should sit in the congregation along with adults to witness and celebrate this event. (See appendix B for sample materials relating to baptism.)

Vacation Bible School

We often think of Vacation Bible School (VBS) as a time for children. But in light of teachable moments, VBS takes on a new meaning. It is a teachable moment, a time to connect the entire family—children, preteens, teens, and adults—around a week of fun and learning.

Publishing companies that present a spiral curriculum for VBS are right on target. This way, the entire family studies the same lesson with variations depending on their developmental level. All week, parents and their children can discuss what they are learning. It's an excellent time for everyone to learn and grow spiritually.

Because they want to bring their children, parents who might not otherwise be inclined to attend a Bible study might do so during VBS. What is especially convenient during this entire week of evening classes is to serve sandwiches or a hot meal at the church for people who work. If the schedule of activities (e.g., praise and worship, classes, crafts) begin and end promptly, families can go home at a rel-atively reasonable hour. Fellowship around food plus fun activities usually equals an unforgettable week.

The following account comes from our VBS director, La Roya Jordan. It demonstrates that the impact of this week can extend well beyond the children.

It was our third year of Vacation Bible School. We were having a wonderful time! The menu for the night was barbecue chicken, mashed potatoes, and corn, and people were eating, talking, and enjoying themselves tremendously.

Just before we were ready to dismiss students to their classes, a lady walked up to me and pulled on my apron. "Are you the one who makes the announcements every night?" she asked. "I just have to tell you something."

I stopped what I was doing and braced myself, fully expecting to hear a complaint. She did not complain. Instead what I heard is something I will never, never forget.

"I want to thank you so much for Vacation Bible School! I have not been this close to God since I was a little kid back in Mississippi," she said with a beaming smile.

I nearly dropped my serving dishes. This woman was at least 70 years old!

As a footnote, it's gratifying and rewarding to hear such praise reports because we don't often realize the effect that our ministry has on the people we serve. In the magazine business, one letter is said to represent nine other people who did not write. So multiply every compliment by ten!

Other ideas for capitalizing on teachable moments include, but are not limited to, reading through the Bible, starting a reader's circle, developing specialized classes for women, teaching through the ministry of song, and developing a ministry for the deaf. Brief explanations of these ministries follow.

Reading Through the Bible

The goal of Christian education is to encourage believers to study the Word. Study begins with reading! In churches that have an annual

"Read Through the Bible" ministry, more people *probably* read the Bible than in churches without this ministry.

Providing a reading schedule and holding a weekly, monthly, quarterly, or semiannual forum to answer questions is all that it takes to launch this ministry. At year's end, because adults like rewards too, it is inspiring to recognize those who actually complete the reading. Having lunch together and awarding "Read Through the Bible Certificates" is one way of congratulating those who persevere.

Reader's Circle

What's at the top of the bestseller list? You guessed it . . . a teachable moment! In every church, many people love to relax by reading. These are the people who would enjoy being a part of a church's "Reader's Circle."

This ministry identifies books, both Christian and secular, and makes recommendations. Individuals can then purchase their own book, read it, and then meet to discuss the book from a biblical perspective. Since biblical knowledge is essential to adequate analysis and evaluation, readers may be challenged to dig more deeply into the Bible. Lively discussions are bound to follow.

Titus 2 Sisters

Dating, engagement, and marriage are times when women are eager to learn how to be wives. That's the ministry of Titus 2 Sisters. In accordance with Scripture, they teach, advise, and counsel young women who are dating, who want to be married, are married, or who are separated from their husbands.

> Likewise, teach the older women to be reverent in the way they live, not to be slanderers or addicted to much wine, but to teach what is good. Then they can train the younger women to love their husbands and children, to be self-controlled and pure, to be busy at home, to be kind, and to be subject to their husbands, so that no one will malign the word of God.
>
> —TITUS 2:3–5

The women who lead such a group—and shared leadership is recommended—should be exemplary models of godly women who love their husbands and children. Deaconesses are the perfect pool from which to select teachers and leaders for this class.

The Ministry of Song

As a postscript to identifying teachable moments for adults, here is a word about the ministry of song. Though we sometimes underestimate its capacity to "teach," singing is perhaps one of the most powerful teaching tools available.

Like the preaching of the Word, singing touches us deep in our emotions. We expect to learn through the ministry of the Word, but we also learn through the ministry of song. Therefore, the words we sing should have the Word of God as their foundation. Since God's Word changes us, songs based on Scripture also have the ability to transform us.

Singing Scripture is powerful. In fact, songs are so important, the Bible has gathered together 150 of them—the book of Psalms! Thus, we can teach by singing Scripture.

As the Deer

As the deer panteth for the water,
So my soul longeth after Thee!
You alone are my heart's desire,
And I long to worship Thee!
You alone are my strength, my shield,
To You alone does my spirit yield.
You alone are my heart's desire,
And I long to worship Thee!

—Martin Nystrom
Based on Psalm 42

Holy Hands

Deaf ears can also learn through the ministry of song and the Word of God. Hands that speak to deaf ears are indeed holy hands!

Here is an area of ministry that will grow by nature of its very existence. Like an announcement broadcast on the village drum, the word spreads quickly among this close-knit community when the church makes specialized services available for the deaf. How wonderful to help them "hear" the Gospel.

A ministry for the deaf is one that demands signers and interpreters who are skilled. It's better to have no signers or interpreters than to have unskilled people who communicate poorly. The deaf become frustrated and feel insulted when they cannot understand. Local colleges and universities offer beginner, intermediate, and advanced classes that test levels of proficiency.

When beginning this ministry, remember that sign language is a language all its own. Just as it takes years for an English-speaking person to master Spanish or French, it takes years to master the art of interpreting.

An effective Holy Hands Ministry reaches beyond signing and into the deaf community. Those who are called to serve in front of the church must also be called to minister behind the scenes. Without involvement with the deaf in their own culture, interpreters will never perfect their skills and the deaf will never truly experience the impact of the life-changing Gospel of Jesus Christ.

Do You Remember?

In this chapter we evaluated the importance of capitalizing on teachable moments as we teach adults. Here is a summary of major points to remember.

- *Voluntary Learners*. Adults are voluntary learners who enter the learning environment when they are motivated to meet needs. This is called teachable moments.

- *The Everyday and Ordinary*. Jesus met his learners in the everyday, ordinary contexts of their lives. When we understand needs, we can better identify teachable moments.

- *College-aged Students*. Some of their needs include finding the right school, job, or career, and living independently.

- *Postcollege-aged Adults*. Some of their needs include choosing careers, finding jobs, and establishing meaningful relationships.

- *Middle-aged Adults*. For those who are 35 to 55, some of their needs include creating a legacy for the next generation.

- *Late Adulthood*. For those who are 55 and over, some of their needs include redefining career or family, transitioning out of the workforce, adjusting to physical changes, preparing for retirement, and helping with or caring for grandchildren.

- *Bible Study, Seminars, and Workshops.* Traditional Bible study, seminars, and workshops are additional ways to teach adults.
- *Disequilibrium.* Learners experience disequilibrium when they experience the unexpected. In teaching, tension can be a positive.
- *Baby Dedication and Baptism.* These specially designed classes are examples of teachable moments that can help adults make important spiritual decisions.
- *Read Through the Bible and Reader's Circle.* By providing a schedule to read through the Bible, educational ministries can encourage the church to read. Evaluating books from a Christian perspective in the context of a "Reader's Circle" is a creative way to dig deeper into the Word.
- *Vacation Bible School.* Traditionally geared for children, VBS is especially beneficial for adults. Providing meals and ending on time encourage attendance.
- *Titus 2 Sisters.* Dating, engagement, and marriage are teachable moments. In this class, the older women teach the younger women according to Titus 2:3–5.
- *Ministry of Song.* Since we also teach through song, singing Scripture can be very powerful.
- *Holy Hands.* This ministry provides quality ministry to the deaf using skilled interpreters who are also involved in the deaf community.

At Journey's End

We have come full circle from examining the teaching methods of Jesus in Part 1 to identifying practical ways to apply Christian education for children, teenagers, and adults in Part 2. As we've seen, there's a great deal of work to do!

Teaching like Jesus, the greatest Teacher of all, guarantees that our task will be rewarding. Throughout this book, we have highlighted important aspects modeled by the Master Teacher. Do you remember? Review the chart on the following page.

THE TEACHER

Jesus taught based on his character.
Jesus understood the learner.

THE LEARNER

Jesus taught developmentally.
Jesus used teachable moments.

TIME AND ENVIRONMENT

Jesus was sensitive to time.
Jesus capitalized on the environment.

THE CURRICULUM

Jesus considered cultural needs.
Jesus appealed to mind, emotions, and behavior.

METHODOLOGY

Jesus involved the senses.
Jesus addressed social concerns.

Just as Jesus taught 12 men in three years and in the end was betrayed by one, denied by another, and deserted by the rest, we won't see positive results overnight. When you feel tired, when ministry doesn't seem worth the effort any longer, when any kind of work seems easier than working in the church, remember Nehemiah. And, don't come off the wall!

Chapter 10

Stay on the Wall!
What to Do When You Feel
Like Quitting

Objective

By the end of this chapter, you will decide to continue in the ministry to which you have been called by evaluating the purpose of your calling.

My father was dying. I stood beside his bed looking into his eyes and holding his hand. When the background music of a commercial played Bette Midler's "Wind Beneath My Wings," we both looked up toward the television. The song put the emotions I was feeling for my dad into words that I was incapable of expressing. It was as if God knew that my heart ached and my throat choked with a lifetime of love.

For much of my early childhood, due to my mother's mental illness, my dad was both father and mother. As the oldest, I clung to him. Since I felt responsible for my sister and brother while dad was at work, his presence gave me the greatest sense of relief, comfort, and safety. Eventually my parents divorced, and my father raised us.

Daddy taught me how to braid my hair, gave me the first compliment I ever received from a man, insisted that we read three or four books every summer, and had time to read everything I wrote. He was my hero, my idol.

Once, when I was sick in the hospital, I remember my father standing by my bedside praying for me. The doctors told him to stay back, but he refused. I was too young to understand what was happening, but I knew that everyone else was afraid, and that frightened me. Daddy pushed past the curtains, came close, held my hands, and prayed. And now, I stood holding his hands . . . praying.

"May I take him now?" the Lord seemed to ask. "Precious in the sight of the Lord is the death of his saints."

"Yes, Lord."

My father had been sick with a heart condition for over 15 years. Every year the doctors thought that he would die, and every year God defied the doctors' prognosis, and Daddy lived. Ten years earlier when my father wore the "death mask"—that ashen complexion we often see on the faces of people who are dying—the Holy Spirit woke me up very early one morning to pray. I opened my Bible to Psalm 90:10, knelt by my bedside, and pleaded with God to extend my dad's life. I knew that I was praying God's will, because the Holy Spirit had prompted me to pray in the first place, and he had given me the Scripture.

"May I take him now? Precious in the sight of the Lord is the death of his saints."

"Yes, Lord."

My husband, Irving, and I had to catch a plane to return home. We had come to visit my father in Atlanta where he was now living under the watchful eye of my brother, Allen, and we had been there for over a week. Irving stood by patiently waiting for me to let go of my father's hand. I thought of our wedding, when again he waited for me to let go of my father's arm.

Daddy was determined to attend the wedding, but he was too weak to travel by plane. He flew anyway. When they touched down in Los Angeles from New York, the flight attendants, visibly relieved, delivered Dad to us on a stretcher. "Your dad's a very sick man!" they remarked in reprimand.

"Well, I'm here," Daddy said to me with a playful smile and mischievous twinkle in his eye. He knew very well that he had defied his doctors by flying three thousand miles in the first place. "I'm not in great shape, but I'm here."

To me, that was all that mattered. My Daddy was here! He couldn't walk me down the aisle, so my Uncle David, tall and stately, did the honors. Dad stood at the front of the church waiting. Once near the altar, I took his arm and held it tightly. As always, my dad was there for every major event in my life. And no matter how difficult it was for him, he was here now.

"Who giveth this woman?" the pastor asked. Dad slipped his hand into the air. "I do." With that, he took a deep breath as if he had just accomplished a major task. And he had! In that moment, all of my little girl dreams had come true. A handsome groom stood by my side, and my father approvingly blessed our marriage.

"Thank you, Daddy," I said. But I didn't feel as if I had said enough, so I stood there—my eyes big with tears—looking at him and holding his arm, the little girl in me not wanting to let go. My husband-to-be took my hand and gave me a loving, gentle tug as he did now. "We're going to miss our plane."

Once again I am looking into Dad's eyes. I hear the background music. "You are the wind beneath my wings. . . ."

Earlier in the day, I asked God if I could cancel my flight home and remain in Atlanta with my dad. There was, however, one minor appointment that I would miss—our annual church meeting. During this Saturday morning, ministries presented their accomplishments for the year to the general congregation. I had prepared a slide presentation of the Children's Ministry for this, my first full year serving the church in the area of Christian education. It was the only reason that I had to go home. Had I decided to stay, surely everyone would have understood that I wanted to spend these last precious moments with my dad.

I asked God if I could stay here with my father. He answered,

> "If anyone comes to me and does not hate his father and mother, his wife and children, his brothers and sisters—yes, even his own life—he cannot be my disciple." —LUKE 14:26

Hate my father? These words echoed loudly in my mind. Such strong words! How could I *hate* my father? In retrospect, I knew why God didn't remind me of the similar, more gentle passage in Matthew 10:37. My love for my dad was so strong that he had to match it with an emotion—hating—that was equally intense.

I told Daddy that I would return as soon as I had made the presentation. When I kissed him goodbye, I honestly thought that I would see him alive again. It wasn't until we were actually settled on the plane that I realized I had seen my father for the last time. Like a revelation, I suddenly understood the pained look in his eyes when I turned around to wave at the door of the hospital room. Daddy was watching me leave, and he was starting to cry, so he turned his head.

When I saw what he was saying in his eyes—that he was telling me good-bye for the last time—I felt a pain so deep that it had to be my heart breaking. My husband held me close as I sobbed and sobbed.

That experience underscored to me that ministry is a priority with God. The ministry report and slide presentation were not minor to him. They were major! So when the slide projector jammed and threatened to ruin my day, I put my hands on my hips and literally spoke to it aloud. "I left my dying father to come here to show this presentation. You *will* work today!"

And it did. Daddy died peacefully in his sleep a few days later.

Hating Father

Of course, the Lord is not commanding hatred. This literary method of hyperbole or exaggeration is necessary to place his perspective above our personal priorities.

> "In the same way, any of you who does not give up everything he has cannot be my disciple." —LUKE 14:33

This charge is not just for pastors, teachers, or volunteers. It is for everyone who names the name of Jesus Christ as Savior. Discipleship demands that we present our entire lives completely, and nothing less will do.

> "And anyone who does not carry his cross and follow me cannot be my disciple." —LUKE 14:27

The second part of this commitment is a willingness to carry our cross . . . to suffer. It's at this point that many pull away. For those of us in ministry, how do we respond when life gets so tough that quitting seems like a sensible option, or when we are so badly wounded that another career—any other career!—seems like a really great idea?

Discouragement, exhaustion, burnout, and battle scars from the front line of ministry are some reasons that we pull away from God and subsequently from his people. We want to avoid being so visible that we attract the enemy's attack. We don't want to be targeted anymore. We don't want to suffer. In short, we don't want to carry our cross.

When we are tempted to put down our cross, it's because we've counted the cost of discipleship and have determined that our bottom line has come up short. Suffering for Jesus just does not seem worth it any longer. The hours are too long, the fruit difficult to see. What difference will one less worker make to the kingdom?

So we leave the work unfinished. Jesus compares this person to a contractor who leaves his building half built.

"Suppose one of you wants to build a tower. Will he not first sit down and estimate the cost to see if he has enough money to complete it? For if he lays the foundation and is not able to finish it, everyone who sees it will ridicule him, saying, 'This fellow began to build and was not able to finish.'"

—LUKE 14:28–30

This fellow was unable to finish because his estimate of the job was incorrect. Hardship was *added.* Instead, it should have been *multiplied!*

Not completing the work is compared by Jesus to salt that has lost its savor.

"Salt is good, but if it loses its saltiness, how can it be made salty again? It is fit neither for the soil nor for the manure pile; it is thrown out.

"He who has ears to hear, let him hear."

—LUKE 14:34–35

Imagine not being good enough even for the manure pile! Unfinished work is worthless. It doesn't count. It is thrown away. Like saltless salt, it is simply good for nothing.

As teachers of the Gospel, we have such a great calling. We are fulfilling the commission to make disciples, to make learners. We minister in obedience to God Almighty. What on earth could possibly force us to leave the work of the ministry?

When tragedy hit, I marveled at my Aunt Lorraine Springsteen. She will never know how her persistence in service to Canaan Baptist Church in New York City modeled to me the true meaning of faithfulness.

Babies aren't supposed to be beautiful when they are born, but Aunt Lorraine and Uncle David's son looked like an angel. The first grandchild, he was absolutely adorable, and we all took our turns spoiling him. I took delight in shopping for him and one Christmas bought him an adorable navy blue sailor set.

Earlier, little David had developed allergic bronchitis. His dad was away on a work assignment, and as a precaution his mom decided to take David to the hospital for treatment of what appeared to be a viral infection. The doctors recommended that he remain overnight for observation. They discouraged anyone from staying in the room with him overnight and urged his mother and grandmother to go home, get rest, and return in the morning, when he would be released.

I was at home with my parents when the telephone rang. "He's gone!" was the hysterical cry from the other end of the wire. This little child had thrown up during the night, and with no one there to assist him, he had choked. In a panic, we drove to the hospital hoping this report to be some mistake. When we arrived, my aunt, slumped over and looking as if her very own spirit had left her, was being pushed out of the hospital in a wheelchair by her husband.

How do you bury your firstborn? The service was grand; the coffin tiny. My aunt, barely able to stand, couldn't lift her head. She had cried so much that I thought heaven's jars would overflow with her tears. Her husband, trying to be strong for his wife, choked on his own enormous grief.

"Yes, Jesus loves me!" This favorite Sunday school song, sung in magnificent tribute to our little David, echoed throughout the church reaffirming God's love. In the midst of such sorrow, the character of our Savior remained intact. He loves us still.

Here is where my aunt's example influenced my life. Rather than leaving her post at the church, she went back to work. The thought of leaving probably never crossed her mind, but I wondered why she stayed. Didn't she feel that God had let her down? Wasn't she angry with God because he allowed this to happen? With all of her service, didn't God owe her more than this?

Instead, without fanfare or loud declarations, my aunt echoed in her attitude the sentiments of Jesus in the Garden of Gethsemane: "Shall I not drink the cup the Father has given me?" (John 18:11).

Today, more than thirty years later, she is still serving in the church. During that time, having earned a graduate degree in clinical social work, she has developed several outreach and social service programs in the church. She supervises the church office, coordinates day-to-day activities, and coordinates the speaking schedule of the senior pastor, Dr. Wyatt Tee Walker.

In a recent conversation, I asked her if she did not at least want a title change—something like assistant to the pastor? "What greater honor can I have and what greater satisfaction can I derive than just giving service?" she answered.

Faithfulness to God . . . humility in service. Sometimes life's lessons speak volumes.

Faithful with a Few Things

How often do we pray, God, give us *this* responsibility, and we'll show the world our gifts and talents! If only we could do *that,* we'd really show them how it should be done!

So often in ministry, we want to do the spectacular. Unless it comes along, we sit passively by, thinking it's someone else's responsibility to do the little things. Years pass, and we wonder why promotion hasn't knocked on our door.

> "Well done, good and faithful servant! You have been faithful with a few things; I will put you in charge of many things. Come and share your master's happiness."
>
> —MATTHEW 25:21

Faithful with few things is where Christian service begins. Coveting the glitter and the glamour just so that we can be seen shows our true motive for Christian service. Unfortunately, we have brought into the church the world's mentality of scrambling to the top any way we can. Foot-washing servants are a premium.

A former professor once told me, "A lot would be accomplished if we didn't care who got the credit." Isn't this statement simply profound? How well are we completing our assignments when no one is looking? How consistent are we when no one keeps a record?

In the few things God has given us, let's fulfill our assignment. And when it becomes difficult to serve, remember Jesus.

Remember Jesus

Remember Jesus. The Jews sought to kill him at the *beginning* of his ministry. According to Luke 4:54, Jesus had only performed two miracles. But by Luke 5:16, his name was already on the Pharisees' hit list.

We are called to follow in his steps (1 Peter 2:21). We will suffer. But isn't this every disciple's prayer?

> I want to know Christ and the power of his resurrection and the fellowship of sharing in his sufferings, becoming like him in his death, and so, somehow, to attain to the resurrection from the dead.
>
> —PHILIPPIANS 3:10–11

We can be certain that, like Jesus, we may also be on someone's hit list. How blessed are we to share in his sufferings. We identify with Christ! We are becoming more like Jesus!

And know this also. With the fellowship of his sufferings is the power of his resurrection. Suffering and crucifixion did not prevent Jesus from rising from the dead. In fact, suffering and crucifixion made resurrection possible. Like Jesus, we will know the power of his resurrection after we suffer with him! Isn't that a great promise?

Jesus glorified the Father. How?

> "I have brought you glory on earth by completing the work you gave
> me to do." —JOHN 17:4

What is the work that God has given you? This is a question that my pastor often asks the staff. He reminds us that there may be other work that is very noble, and there may be other causes that are really worth championing. Of themselves, these jobs, these causes may be quite good, perhaps even praiseworthy. But is that what God has asked *you* to do? This catchy saying, my grandmother's favorite, measures earthly options by the yardstick of eternity.

> Only one life
> 'Twill soon be past;
> Only what's done for Christ will last.

Be faithful in little, and finish the work! That's it. That's what God wants us to do. Why do we give up? Why do we quit? At Youth for Christ's annual summer leadership retreat for youth workers, one speaker—Tony Williams, pastor of the Maranatha Christian Church in San Jose, California—explained the three reasons we leave our work incomplete: the enemy, "church folk," and circumstances. With a heavenly perspective, he exhorted us to "stay on the wall."

You're Doing a Great Work!

Remember Nehemiah? He was doing a great work (Neh. 6:3). But he experienced opposition. First, there was Sanballat, a name that, like the Devil, speaks of hatred. Then there was Tobiah, who represents religious people who don't want us to accomplish *too* much. And finally, there was Geshem, whose name means "hard rain," which represents the common, unexpected, and difficult circumstances in our lives.

These enemies taunted Nehemiah daily as he endeavored to rebuild the wall at Jerusalem. They were always urging him to quit. They ridiculed him; they threatened him. They tried to embarrass Nehemiah, and they tried to belittle him.

The Devil is relentless in his efforts to force you to quit. He is persistent—he *never* gives up! He is intimidating, but he's a liar. His ultimate goal is to weaken your hand, to strip you of your power.

He wants you to come down and go to the valley of Ono (Neh. 6:2). But tell him, "Oh, no! I won't come down!" Be like Nehemiah. Don't come off the wall!

In order to stay on the wall, you must know that you're doing a *great work*. Ministry to the Lord, ministry to the body of Christ, and ministry to the lost and hurting is an upward calling. Don't come down!

What a wonderful exhortation from Pastor Williams! But how do we stay on the wall? Let's return to Jesus, the Master Teacher. It all begins with him.

Renew Your Love

It's time to renew your love. Think back to the beginning. Remember singing, "Amazing grace, how sweet the sound, that saved a wretch like me," and wanting to announce to everyone, "I'm the wretch who was saved by grace"?

Remember the gratitude, the fire? When you evaluate where you are now, has that spark dimmed? Has the vision faded? Have you lost your first love?

Renew by spending time alone with God and his Word. Renew by telling God where you are, where you hurt, and how you feel. Renew by surrounding yourself with godly men and women who will encourage you and pray for you. Get recharged. Get energized. Then keep on going and going and going!

Retreat Quarterly

How did Jesus finish his work? Jesus often pulled away from the crowds to be alone with the Father. Time and time again he left the disciples and the multitudes to pray and rest.

So often we become so engrossed in ministry that we neglect our time alone with the Father. There's so much work to do. We are just too busy! Isn't it amazing that God himself did not try to heal everyone all the time? Yet we find it difficult to spend even a day to commune with the One we serve.

Personal retreats are a must for maintaining our saltiness. Prayer, praise, fasting, and solitude are necessary ingredients for a meaningful

Leader's Tip

It's vital to encourage your teachers and volunteers. Here are a few suggestions:

- *Celebrate Often.* An annual Christmas dinner says, "Thank you," to those who have worked so unselfishly all year. The church should sponsor the dinner for each teacher and spouse or guest. They will love it if this occasion is formal, so that everyone gets a chance to dress up! Entertainment is inexpensive if you allow the teachers themselves to perform.

- *Retreat Annually.* Every summer take the volunteer staff on a retreat where they can be recharged and refreshed. This is a wonderful time for leaders to mingle one-on-one with their staff, to engage in casual conversation, and just to have fun.

- *Take Pictures.* When you stop by during class and take pictures of your teachers, volunteers, and students, you are telling them that they are special. Post pictures, circulate them in teachers' meetings, share them with your pastor and church staff. Let others know the people who are working behind the scenes.

- *Send Flowers.* Visiting them in the hospital and sending cards and flowers when they are ill says you care. It's an expense that should be included in every Christian education budget.

- *Remember the Adults.* Sometimes the adult Bible study teachers feel forgotten. We focus so much energy on those who work with children that the faithful adult teachers receive few "Thank-yous." Include them in your Christmas celebration and summer retreat. Sit in on their Bible studies, and call periodically to see that they have everything they need.

- *Call Spontaneously.* Call just to say, "Hello, how are you?" Ask about the children, spouse, and job. Find a commonality between you and your volunteers that extends beyond the church walls.

- *Feed Your Staff.* At every opportunity, feed your teachers! Provide snacks, coffee, and juice on Sunday morning. Have snacks at your monthly teachers' meetings since most volunteers are coming to church straight from work. Fellowship around these meal times can be very refreshing! Your teachers will know that you—and God—are always thinking about them.

life of service. Those involved in ministry on a daily basis should retreat often—once every three months if at all possible. This means that every year we will plan to spend four entire days alone with God.

Rejoice Daily

Praise God for the cross, and praise him for sharing in his suffering. Praise him for the religious people who irritate us like sand does the pearl, only to produce in our lives rare and exquisite beauty. Praise him for the difficult circumstances we experience that make us more compassionate to the people whom we serve.

And praise him for the joy of ministry. It's not *all* suffering *all* of the time. Thank God for the laughter, for the victories, for the ones won to Christ. Rejoice! There is strength for today. Rejoice! There is victory to come. Rejoice! The work is being done. Every day, find reasons to rejoice.

Jesus Prayed for You

Jesus prayed for you. On his way to the cross, Jesus paused, looked down the road to eternity, and saw you, his disciple. In full knowledge of the challenges facing you, Jesus prayed just for you.

> "I am coming to you now, but I say these things while I am still in the world, so that they may have the full measure of my joy within them. I have given them your word and the world has hated them, for they are not of the world any more that I am of the world. My prayer is not that you take them out of the world but that you protect them from the evil one. They are not of the world, even as I am not of it. Sanctify them by the truth; your word is truth. As you sent me into the world, I have sent them into the world. For them I sanctify myself, that they too may be truly sanctified.
>
> "My prayer is not for them alone. I pray also for those who will believe in me through their message, that all of them may be one, Father, just as you are in me and I am in you. May they also be in us so that the world may believe that you have sent me. I have given them the glory that you gave me, that they may be one as we are one: I in them and you in me. May they be brought to complete unity to let the world know that you sent me and have loved them even as you have loved me."
>
> —John 17:13–23

So Send I You

So send I you—to labor unrewarded,
To serve unpaid, unloved, unsought, unknown,
To bear rebuke, to suffer scorn and scoffing—
So send I you, to toil for Me alone.

So send I you—to bind the bruised and broken,
O'er wand'ring souls to work, to weep, to wake,
To bear the burdens of a world a-weary—
So send I you, to suffer for My sake.

So send I you—to loneliness and longing,
With heart a-hung'ring for the loved and known,
Forsaking home and kindred, friend and dear one—
So send I you, to know My love alone.

So send I you—to leave your life's ambition,
To die to dear desire, self-will resign,
To labor long, and love where men revile you—
So send I you, to lose your life in Mine.

So send I you—to hearts made hard by hatred,
To eyes made blind because they will not see,
To spend, tho' it be blood, to spend and spare not—
So send I you, to taste of Calvary.

—E. Margaret Clarkson

Heavenly Rewards

Does our work have eternal value? During a Biola University chapel service, Francis Chan, pastor of the Cornerstone Community Church in Simi Valley, California, challenged students and faculty to store up treasures in heaven. He urged us to reevaluate our motives for ministry. Are we willing to sacrifice and give up our lives, knowing that we will be rewarded in the end?"

We work, we persuade people because judgment is coming. God, in his great love, has already provided a way to save the whole world. Jesus Christ is "the way and the truth and the life" (John 14:6).

Christian teacher, you are vital in reaching the lost in your world. In addition to life abundant and overflowing in the here and now, those you win to Christ have heaven as their eternal destiny.

So teach, for heaven's sake! And for heaven's sake, teach!

"Behold, I am coming soon! My reward is with me, and I will give to everyone according to what he has done."

—REVELATION 22:12

Appendix A
Sample Lessons

Sample Lessons

Eight sample lessons from teacher volunteers and former students are included in this section. They are written for a variety of cultures and age groups as indicated in each lesson.

The goal of this section is to model how to creatively apply "Hook, Book, Look, Took" as you write your own lessons. (Some lessons also include Wanda Parker's "Nook" and Dr. Shelly Cunningham's "Cook.") Each step of Bloom's Taxonomy is covered in one of these lessons as indicated *in brackets* following the objective.

Remember that writing good lessons takes practice! Often, *after* you teach a lesson, ways to improve it become immediately obvious. Make a note of these ideas because like a good sermon, a good lesson can be taught again and again.

Leader's Tip

Ask your teachers to review the following lesson plans and evaluate them by answering:

- What works?
- What doesn't work?
- What's missing?

Lesson Plan 1

House on a Rock

by Mindy Owes

Objective

By the end of a 15-minute lesson on Matthew 7:24–27, students will remember that God's Word makes us strong by identifying the house that remains standing after the storm. [Knowledge]

For African-American Preschoolers

Materials Checklist

- Bibles
- Flannelgraph

Craft Checklist

- Materials to make toy houses (e.g., a Lego set)
- Two plastic shoe boxes: one to fill with sand and water, the other to fill with rocks and water
- Toy houses to put into the plastic boxes (optional: trees, etc.)
- A watering can for plants (for the rain)

Hook Ask students to describe what they do when it rains. What games do they play indoors? What do they wear to school? During this discussion, teacher may show pictures of children dressed in rain-wear (cut out from magazines). Optional: actually have a raincoat and an umbrella.

> *Bridge:* "Today we are going to learn a story about two houses in the rain."

Book Tell the account with a flannelgraph. (Place the flannelgraph characters inside the pages of your Bible; as you tell the account, remove the characters from your Bible.)

Now ask the students to take turns telling the account again. Let the children place the figures onto the flannelgraph board.

After the students have retold this account, the teacher tells it again, this time using the two plastic boxes as a demonstration—one house is in the box on sand; the other is in a box on top of rocks. Now, using the watering can, pretend that there's a storm and pour water over both houses. Make a *big* sound as the house on the sand crumbles.

Look Tell them that when we study God's Word, God will make us strong.

Note: Children will not understand that our lives are *like* houses—that the people who hear but who do not obey God will ultimately be destroyed—so avoid making this comparison.

Took Help children to identify that the house on the rock was the best house because it did not fall in the storm.

> *Craft:* Make houses out of Lego or similar building blocks.

Lesson Plan 2

Trusting in God

by Sonja Schappert

Objective

By the end of a 30-minute lesson on the account of Noah (Genesis 6–8), students will recall that Noah trusted in God, by drawing a scene from the account. [Knowledge]

For Caucasian Five-Year-Olds (Kindergarten)

Nook Play Christian music for children to set a worship atmosphere in the classroom. As parents drop off their children, have toys out for them to play with until the lesson begins. When it is time to start the lesson, ask the students to put away their toys and help them put the toys into the correct bins. Put stickers on the backs of the hands of those children who are helping to put away the toys. Encourage everyone to participate. Open with prayer for the students and ask them how they are doing.

Hook (5 minutes)

Bridge: "Today we are going to learn an exciting lesson from God's Word. Let's begin by singing a song."

Ask the students to stand. Play the song "Arky Arky" (lyrics enclosed). Have a couple of children hold the poster with the words on it. Lead the students in the song and teach them the hand motions. After the song is over, have the children gather for the lesson.

Book (10 minutes)

Bridge: "Now it is time to hear a Bible account about a man who trusted in God."

Help the children open their Bibles to Genesis 6 before telling the account. Tell the class that you will need helpers to tell it (to place the flannelgraph pieces), so if they sit quietly, you will call on them to help you.

Materials Checklist

- Animal stickers
- "Arky Arky" from recording of *Psalty Kids' Praise* 2 (published by Word Music)
- Tape player
- Flannelgraph board and easel
- Flannelgraph characters for Noah's ark placed in a Bible (available from *Bible in Felt*, revised 1992, published by Little Folks Visuals, Palm Desert, CA, lessons 6 and 7)
- Spray bottle with water
- Animal crackers and diluted apple juice for snack
- Napkins and paper cups
- White drawing paper
- Chubby crayons
- Optional: an audio version of the Noah account, from *The Bible in Living Sound*, Tape #3, Norland, Washington

Craft Checklist

- Make a poster with the words as sung to "Arky Arky."
- Prepare the art supplies for craft time.
- Pour the apple juice into cups and have the animal crackers ready to eat.
- Cue up the tape for "Arky Arky."

A long time ago there was a man named Noah. *[Have a child take the figure of Noah from the pages of your Bible and place it on the flannel board.]* Noah was a good man who knew and obeyed God. *[Ask another student to begin placing the other people in the story.]*

God looked down from heaven and saw that everyone on earth was evil. They did not love God. But Noah and his family did. Noah loved God. So God said to Noah, "I am going to make new people" (Genesis 6:13). Then God told Noah to build a great big boat, called an ark, because there was going to be a flood. *[Have the ark placed on the flannel board.]* But God promised Noah that he and his family would be safe.

Noah trusted God that he would be protected from the flood. Then God told Noah to put two of every kind of animal in the ark so that they, too, would be protected from the flood. *[Have the animals placed on the board.]*

After many, many years the ark was finished. God told Noah that it would rain for 40 days and 40 nights. *[Begin lightly spraying students with water from the spray bottle; don't stop until after the rain has stopped! Place the storm clouds on the flannelgraph board.]* Noah *trusted* that God would keep his family safe, and God did. He shut the great big door of the ark to keep Noah and his family safe from the flood.

[Change the flannelgraph background to the waterscape.]

All the wicked people who did not love God died. Noah *trusted* God for protection from the storm. The only living creatures left on earth were Noah, his family, and the animals on the ark. The earth was under water for a very long time, but after a while the water went away. Soon Noah could see the tops of the mountains. The ark came to rest on Mount Ararat.

Noah sent out a dove to search for land. *[Have a dove placed on the board.]* The dove returned with an olive branch in its mouth. Noah knew then that there was dry ground, and God told Noah that it was time to come out of the ark. Again, Noah *trusted* God. When he and his family went outside, the earth was dry again. *[Put back the dry ground background and place on it some trees, the mountain, and the ark.]* Noah and his family and all the animals came out of the ark. *[Have a student put up the animal figures coming out of the ark.]*

Then Noah built an altar to the Lord. He thanked God for keeping him and his family safe. God promised Noah that he would never destroy the whole earth with a flood again. God put a rainbow in the sky to remind us of his promise.

Lesson Review (2 minutes) As the lesson is reviewed, children may retell the account and place the flannelgraph pictures on the board all over again.

1. Why did God send a flood to the earth? *Because the people were evil and did not love God*
2. How did Noah trust God? *Noah did what God asked him to do. He built the ark and put the pairs of animals inside. Noah trusted in God to protect him and his family*
3. How long did it rain? *Forty days and 40 nights*
4. What kind of bird did Noah send out? *A dove*
5. What was in the dove's mouth when it returned? *An olive branch*
6. Will God ever flood the whole earth again? *No*
7. How can we be sure? *Because God made the rainbow as a promise*

Look (5 minutes) Teach the Bible memory verse: Proverbs 3:5, "Trust in the LORD with all your heart."

Bridge: "Noah trusted God to protect him and his family. Noah showed that he trusted God by following his commands. What are some ways that you can trust God? How can you obey him?"

Help the students come up with ways that they can trust God. (Example: They can trust God to help them obey their parents.)

Took (5 minutes)

Bridge: "Now it's time for you to draw your own pictures about the story of Noah. Come over to the tables and have a seat."

With assistance from parent volunteers, ask each student to draw a picture that shows how Noah trusted or obeyed God. Make sure the students' name are on the picture.

Snack Time (5 minutes) Use this time again for lesson review.

Bridge: "Now it is time to clean up our crayons so that we can have a snack."

Ask for student helpers to pass out napkins. Pass out the animal crackers and ask the names of the different animals. Ask whether these animals were also on the ark. Pass out the apple juice, making sure the cups are only half full so as to avoid spills.

Arky Arky
(with Hand Motions)

The Lord told Noah, there's going to be floody, floody.
[Move arms down in rain motion and up again with flood motion]
Lord told Noah, there's going to be a floody, floody.
[Move arms down in rain motion and up again with flood motion]
Get those animals out of the muddy, muddy,
Children of the Lord.

The Lord told Noah to build Him an arky, arky.
[Make building motions with hands]
Lord told Noah to build Him an arky, arky.
[Make building motions with hands]
Make it out of gopher barky, barky.
Children of the Lord.

Chorus

So rise *[lift arms up]* and shine *[keep arms up, slightly out, palms open]*
And give God the glory, glory *[wave arms back and forth]*,
Rise *[lift arms up]* and shine *[keep arms up, slightly out, palms open]*
And give God the glory, glory *[wave arms back and forth]*,
[With more emphasis] Rise *[lift arms up]* and shine *[keep arms up, slightly out, palms open]*
And give God the glory, glory *[wave arms back and forth]*,
Children of the Lord.

The animals, the animals, they came in by twosy, twosies.
[Two fingers walking up your sloped arm]
Animals, the animals, they came in by twosy, twosies.
[Two fingers walking up your sloped arm]
Elephants and kangaroosies, roosies,
Children of the Lord.

(Chorus)

It rained and poured *[use arms to make rain motions]*
for forty daysies, daysies *[use 10 fingers to count 40]*,
Rained and poured *[use arms to make rain motions]*
for forty daysies, daysies *[use 10 fingers to count 40]*,
Almost drove those animals crazies, crazies,
Children of the Lord.

(Chorus)

The sun came out and dried up the landy, landy *[point to the sky]*,
The sun came out and dried up the landy, landy *[point to the sky]*,
Everything is fine and dandy, dandy,
Children of the Lord.

Lesson Plan 3

An Angel Brings Good News

by Saundra Coleman

Objective

By the end of a 30-minute lesson on Luke 1:5–24, students will recognize that God wants us to have faith by identifying one difficulty they have and praying about that problem. [Knowledge]

For African-American Second-Grade Students

Materials Checklist

- Bibles
- White board and markers

Craft Checklist

- Materials to make angel ornaments

Hook Have you ever wanted something very badly? What was it? If this lesson is taught during the Christmas season, children may list toys or clothes, for example. Discuss their Christmas list, but tell them that we do not always get everything we want.

Bridge: "Today, we are going to study about a husband and wife who wanted something very badly, and God heard their prayers."

Book Ask children to hold up their Bibles. Recite the Bible pledge:

I pledge allegiance to the Bible, God's Holy Word. I will make it a lamp to my feet and a light along my path. I will hide God's Word in my heart that I might not sin against God.

Read Luke 1:13. Using pictures from a picture Bible (or a coloring book), tell this Bible account: Zechariah and his wife wanted to have a baby. They had waited a long, long time, but still they did not have a child of their own. The angel Gabriel appeared to Zechariah to give him the good news. When Zechariah saw the angel, he was afraid. But the angel told him not to be afraid. God had heard his prayers for a child. Zechariah and his wife Elizabeth were going to have a son—John the Baptist—who would tell people about Jesus.

Bridge: "God wants us to believe his Word. The Bible is God's Word, and when we pray, God says that he will help us. I want you to think about one problem that you might have. We are going to pray and ask for God's help."

Look Tell a story about a boy who was having trouble at school. The other kids picked on him and tried to get him to fight. He was very afraid, but he knew what God's Word said. "Never will I leave you; never will I forsake you" (Heb. 13:5b). So he prayed and asked God to help him. An older boy in the fifth grade saw the kids picking on this little boy and made them leave him alone. He told this little boy that if he ever had any more trouble out of them to let him know. God had answered his prayer by sending someone to help.

Took God wants us to trust him. If you are having trouble at school, pray and ask God to help you. Teacher, ask students if there is anything they want you to pray about now. Pray a sentence prayer for each need that is expressed.

Craft: Make angel ornaments.

Lesson Plan 4

If Jesus Came to Your House

by Janice Webb

Objective

By the end of a 45-minute lesson on 1 Thessalonians 4:16, students will explain how they can be ready for Jesus and his return by comparing how their lives would differ if Jesus were to visit them unexpectedly. [Comprehension]

For African-American Third- and Fourth-Grade Students

Materials Checklist

- Bibles
- White board and two contrasting colored markers
- Poem: "If Jesus Came to Your House"

Hook With excitement and without giving the name of the guest, ask your students the following questions and, using one of the colored markers, write their answers on the board.

1. If a very special guest unexpectedly arrived at your home to stay with you for a few days (gender and age are irrelevant), what would be the first thing you would have to do? (Answers may include cleaning up their room by putting toys and books away, hanging up clothes, making the bed, etc.)

2. If your company had to borrow one or two of your favorite outfits, what kind of clothes would that be? (Answers may include sagging pants, designer shoes, or jeans with holes in them. What clothes would you put away?)

3. What kind of books or magazines do you have on your table, desk, or in the bookshelf? Would these be okay for your guest to read? (Answers may include a secret diary, *Power Rangers*, *X-Man*, *Sweet Valley High*, *D.C. Comics*, *High Times*, and the like. What books would you hide?)

4. What type of music would your guest listen to with you? (Discuss radio stations, favorite songs, and favorite recording artists. What songs would you not want your guest to hear? Discuss the lyrics in the songs. What do they make you think of? How do they make you feel?)

5. What "new" words would your guest have to learn? (Discuss favorite slang words, phrases, or greetings. Are there any words you wouldn't say around this guest?)

6. Where would be your favorite places to chill or hang out? (Answers may include the mall, video game parlors, burger stops, school, etc. What places might you avoid?)
7. How would you feel if this special guest met your best friend? (Discuss this friend's habits—language, clothing, music, etc.)

Bridge: "The Bible tells us that Jesus is coming back for us. Will we be ready?"

Book Ask a student to read 1 Thessalonians 4:16. Talk about the "Rapture" and how God is going to take to heaven everyone who believes in him through Jesus Christ. (Since this is the hope of every believer, talk about the Rapture in happy, positive terms. Stress the fact that we want to be ready when he comes. The first step is to know that we are saved.)

Look Ask students how prepared they are if Jesus were to come back today. Read the poem, "If Jesus Came to Your House." Reread the poem and point to the answers on the board from the questions that were asked at the beginning of class. Now, using a different colored marker, what would be changed? Why?

Took Place students in small groups of three or four. Ask them to discuss what they have learned today. Will this make a difference in their lives this week? How? Is there anyone who does not know Jesus Christ as Savior? Why not pray today?

If Jesus Came to Your House

If Jesus came to your house to spend a day or two,
If He came unexpectedly I wonder what you'd do?
Oh, I know you'd give your nicest room to such an
    honored Guest,
And all the food you'd serve to Him would be the very best,
And you would keep assuring Him you're glad to have Him there,
That serving Him in your own home is joy beyond compare.

But when you saw Him coming, would you meet Him at the door
With arms outstretched in welcome to your Heavenly Visitor?
Or would you have to change your clothes before you let Him in?
Or hide some magazines and put the Bible where they'd been?
Would you turn off the radio and hope He hadn't heard?
And wish you hadn't uttered that last, loud, hasty word?

Would you hide your worldly music and put some
    hymnbooks out?
Could you let Jesus walk right in or would you rush about?
And I wonder if the Savior spent a day or two with you,
Would you go right on doing the things you always do?
Would you go right on saying the things you always say?
Would life for you continue as it does from day to day?

Would your family conversation keep up its usual pace?
And would you find it hard each meal to say a table grace?
Would you sing the songs you always sing and read the
    books you read?
And let Him know the things on which your mind and
    spirit feed?
Would you take Jesus with you everywhere you had planned
    to go?
Or would you, maybe, change your plans for just a day or so?

Would you be glad to have Him meet your very closest friends?
Or would you hope they'd stay away until His visit ends?
Would you be glad to have Him stay forever on and on?
Or would you sigh with great relief when He at last was gone?
It might be interesting to know the things that you would do
If Jesus Christ came in person to spend some time with you!

—Author Unknown

Lesson Plan 5

"Sabio" Means Wise

by John Lewis

Objective

By the end of an hour lesson on Matthew 7:24–27, students will decide how to make wise decisions by solving a problem based on the acrostic, SABIO. [Evaluation]

For Sixth Graders at the Hispanic Ministry Center

Hook Select five girls and five boys. Allow two minutes for them to build a house out of marshmallows. The goal is to build the houses as tall and as solid as possible. When the two minutes are up, count the layers of the house and declare the winner. Select another four volunteers (two boys and two girls) to help during your lesson. One boy and one girl have squirt bottles for "rain," and the others will use cardboard to "blow" whenever the word "wind" is mentioned.

Bridge: "When we obey Jesus, the Bible tells us that we are like 'a wise man who built his house on the rock.'"

Book Ask students to open their Bibles to Matthew 7:24–27. In small groups, read these verses. What is similar between these two houses? (Answer: Everyone hears.) What is different? (Answer: Only one person obeys.)

Bridge: "The house that was built on the sand is like these marshmallow houses. As we read the passage together this time, let's see which team's house falls first."

Now, ask one student to read Matthew 7:27 out loud. Be sure that the rain and wind volunteers (they may even have a sign that tells the class what part of nature they are playing) are alert to respond when their parts are mentioned. "The rain came down *[squirt water on both houses]*, the streams rose, and the wind blew *[wave cardboard on both houses]* and beat against that house, and it fell with a great crash" (Matt. 7:27).

Materials Checklist

- Bibles
- Marshmallows
- SABIO poster (definition/process) and slips of paper that explain SABIO
- Two squirt bottles
- Two pieces of cardboard
- Poster board
- Lesson notes

Craft Checklist

- Rocks (Don't even think about throwing them!)
- Paint and brushes, letters or stickers, to decorate SABIO rocks

Look In what ways do boys and girls your age make decisions today? Suggestions may include listening to their friends, parents, making decisions on their own, getting advice from television, and so on. Let students brainstorm.

> *Bridge:* "Does any of this advice help us to obey God? The Bible will help us to be wise, just like the person who built his house on a rock. Let's use the word 'wise' or SABIO, to help us when we have a decision to make."

S: The S in SABIO stands for SITUACIÓN—*What is the problem?* State the problem in the simplest, most specific way. Answer: Who? What? When? Where?

A: The A in SABIO stands for ACCIONES—*What action can I take?* What options do I have? Is there anything else I can try? List both good and bad options.

B: The B in SABIO stands for BENEFICIOS—*What's right with the actions I could take?* What's wrong with the actions I could take? (Teacher: Help the students look at the pros and cons of each option.) What are your thoughts about these actions. Review the advantages and disadvantages (beneficios/desventajas).

I: The I in SABIO stands for INVITA A DIOS—*Pray about what to do.* Always ask God what he would want you to do. What does the Bible say about this situation?

O: The O in SABIO stands for ¡O!—*Oh! I know what I should do!* This is when you decide which action to take. Which decision is in keeping with God's Word?

Took Ask students to get into small groups. What kinds of situations do they face in which they may need help making the right decision? Take one of these examples and apply SABIO. Give each group slips of paper with the explanation for SABIO to use as a reference. Report back to the class at large.

S:	Situación	What's the problem?
A:	Acciones	What actions can they take?
B:	Beneficios	What's right/wrong with the actions you could take?
I:	Invita a Dios	Pray. Read your Bible.
O:	¡O!	Choose what you are going to do.

Craft: Make SABIO rocks. These rocks are to remind us of the man who built his house on the rock. Let the children select and decorate their own rocks to keep to remind them how to make wise decisions.

Lesson Plan 6

I Am God's Workmanship
by Karen Choi

Objective

By the end of a 45-minute lesson on Ephesians 2:10, students will decide whether or not they are God's workmanship by evaluating their gifts and talents. [Evaluation]

Note: This lesson is organized according to Bloom's Taxonomy. (See brackets.)

For Korean Junior High School Girls

Hook Display a picture from one of the art books. [Knowledge]

Bridge: "What do you see?" (Allow students to have a short discussion on artists they know and about the paintings with which they are familiar. Display a painting with which everyone is familiar, like Mona Lisa, so that students feel good about themselves for recognizing a work of art.)

Bridge: "What can you tell me about these paintings?" [Comprehension]

Discuss that they are beautiful, they are treasures, they are priceless, and so on. Just as these great artists created these famous paintings, so God himself created each one of you. How much more valuable are you? We often forget this fact.

Look #1 Ask the young ladies what they usually say when someone compliments them? Mimic how they respond—"Yeah, right!" "Whatever . . ." etc.

Note: "Look" can precede "Book," depending on the lesson.

Bridge: "But are we comparable to these paintings that were made by mere men? Are we masterpieces created by the Ultimate Artist—God himself?" Answer "Yes!" [Application]

Book #1 Read Ephesians 2:10: "For we are God's workmanship, created in Christ Jesus to do good works, which God prepared in

Materials Checklist
- Bibles
- "Miss the Mark" dart game
- Art books with masterpieces by artists such as Monet, Picasso, or Michelangelo. (If you don't have such a book, borrow one from the library.)
- "Who Am I?" handout

Craft Checklist
- Plain paper to make a "Talents List"
- Crayons or colored pencils

advance for us to do." Since this is a short verse, give students time to memorize it; ask them to repeat the verse aloud with others checking for accuracy.

Look #2 Ask students why girls their age don't have good images of themselves. Discuss issues such as peer pressure, comparing ourselves with others, being popular or unpopular, and trying to live up to the images we see on television and in magazines. [Analysis]

Book #2 Stress that our identity lies in Christ. Distribute "Who Am I?" handout [I am a child of God; the righteousness of God in Christ, a new creature, etc.]. Read aloud in unison.

Look #3 How can we solve poor image problems? Discuss practical ways to keep our holy identities intact by doing such things as encouraging our friends, avoiding the habit of "bagging" on each other, meditating on who God says we are in the "Who Am I?" sheet. [Synthesis]

Ask students to list their individual talents. Talents can include everything—not just being good at sports, music, or school, but little things like being a good listener (for instance, talking on the phone), smiling a lot, helping people, and being a good friend.

Distribute the plain paper to make a "Talents List." Have students fold their papers in half lengthwise. On the left side ask them to list their specific talent. On the right, ask them to write what they can *do* with that talent for God. Now have them give one compliment to the person next to them to help start her list. Next, have students share what they wrote down. They may add to their list based on the group's input and discussion. And they may decorate their list with the crayons or colored pencils.

Bridge: "What would happen if we continually remembered the fact that we are God's workmanship created to do good works?" Answers may include being more positive, having more confidence, staying away from bad habits.

Bridge: "Is it better to have this new self-image knowing who we are in Christ? In what one area can you develop more confidence? What is one negative thought that you are going to change to a positive one according to the Word of God?" [Evaluation]

Took Based on the above question, allow students time to think about how they have been living their lives. End in a prayer of thanksgiving that we are God's workmanship, and that each of us is an individual with unique talents and beauty. We have been made in the likeness of God. Ask God to help us to see ourselves as he sees us.

Who Am I?

A child of God (Romans 8:16)

Redeemed from the hand of the enemy (Psalm 107:2)

Forgiven (Colossians 1:13–14)

Saved by grace through faith (Ephesians 2:8)

Justified (Romans 5:1)

Sanctified (1 Corinthians 6:11)

A new creature (2 Corinthians 5:17)

A partaker of Jesus' divine nature (2 Peter 1:4)

Redeemed from the curse of the law (Galatians 3:13)

Delivered from the powers of darkness (Colossians 1:13)

Led by the Spirit of God (Romans 8:14)

A son of God (Romans 8:14)

In the charge of angels (Psalms 91:11)

Assured that as I give, all my needs are met (Philippians 4:19)

Casting all my cares on Jesus (1 Peter 5:7)

Strong in the Lord and in the power of his might (Ephesians 6:10)

Doing all things through Christ who strengthens me (Philippians 4:13)

An heir of God and a joint heir with Jesus Christ (Romans 8:17)

A royal priesthood, a holy nation (1 Peter 2:9)

Doing the Lord's commandments (Luke 6:46–48)

Blessed coming in and blessed going out (Deuteronomy 28:6)

An heir of life eternal (1 John 5:11–12)

Blessed with all spiritual blessings (Ephesians 1:3)

Healed by Jesus' stripes (1 Peter 2:24)

Exercising my authority over the enemy (Luke 10:19)

Content with what I have (Hebrews 13:5)

More than a conqueror (Romans 8:37)

Going into all the world with the Gospel (Mark 16:15)

An overcomer by the blood of the Lamb and the word of my testimony (Revelation 12:11)

Greater than the one who is in the world (1 John 4:4)

Not moved by what I see, but seeing things that are eternal (2 Corinthians 4:18)

Walking by faith and not by sight (2 Corinthians 5:7)

Casting down vain imaginations (2 Corinthians 10:4–5)

Bringing every thought into captivity (2 Corinthians 10:5)

Being transformed by renewing my mind (Romans 12:1–2)

A laborer together with God (1 Corinthians 3:9)

The righteousness of God in Christ (2 Corinthians 5:21)

An imitator of Jesus (Ephesians 5:1)

The light of the world (Matthew 5:14)

Blessing the Lord at all times and continually praising the Lord with my mouth (Psalm 34:1)

Fearfully and wonderfully made (Psalm 139:14)

Heard by the Lord in the day of trouble (Psalm 20:1)

Not walking in the counsel of the wicked (Psalm 1:1)

Delighting in the law of the Lord (Psalm 1:2)

Meditating on God's Word (Psalm 1:2)

Bringing forth fruit in season (Psalm 1:3)

Prospering in whatever I do (Psalm 1:3)

Thirsting for the living God (Psalm 42:2)

Waiting for Jesus' return (1 Thessalonians 4:16)

Lesson Plan 7

Victory over Temptations

by Viken P. Kiledjian

Objective

By the end of a 30-minute lesson on Matthew 4:3–11, students will identify one way to fight temptations by classifying temptations that can be overcome using Jesus' method. [Application]

For Armenian High School Students

Materials Checklist

- Bibles
- White board and markers

Hook In one large group, ask students, "What does the word *temptation* mean?" "What are some common sources of temptation for teenagers?" List the answers on the white board.

Book Read Matthew 4:3–11 and ask students to note the nature of each temptation Jesus faced. Now read 1 John 2:15–17. On the board, categorize the three temptations of Jesus in the three following columns:

1. The cravings of sinful man (lust of the flesh)
2. Lust of the eyes
3. Boasting of what he has and does (pride of life)

Bridge: "Spurgeon, the great Christian theologian, said, 'Earnest Christian men are not so much afraid of trials as of temptations. The great horror of a Christian is sin.' What was Jesus' rebuttal when he was tempted? Upon what were his answers based? How did Jesus' physical discomfort—being hungry—affect his decisions?"

Look Divide students into three equal groups. Ask each group to devise a modern-day scenario of teenage temptations based on one of the three groups listed on the board (one temptation per group). Ask students to develop two endings of the scenario: one where students give in to the temptation and a different ending where students are victorious using the technique modeled by Jesus.

Tᴏᴏᴋ In order to fight temptation, we must know what the Bible says. Ask students, "What else can we do?" (Answers should include prayer, talking to parents, teachers, pastors, or friends.) Discuss the memory verse. Allow students three minutes to pray silently about an area of temptation they may face.

Memorize: Matthew 6:13—"And lead us not into temptation, but deliver us from the evil one."

Lesson Plan 8

The Sacrifice

by Brooke Boersma

Objective

By the end of an hour lesson on Hebrews 9:27–28, students will evaluate the importance of Christ's sacrifice in their own lives by writing their choice to believe in him, recommit to him, or to say "No!" to him. [Evaluation]

For a Group of Multiethnic High School Students (Latino, Dutch Reformed, Anglo, African-American)

Materials Checklist

- Bibles
- Audio/Visual: Michael W. Smith's "Secret Ambition" music video
- TV/VCR
- Lyric slides
- A small altar made of rocks or a facsimile
- Cross necklaces, New Believer packets, power bracelets, "cross in my pocket"
- 3 x 5 cards
- Pens

Hook Tell this story. (Students are seated in a large auditorium.)

———————

There was a guy about your age named Carlos. He grew up in the city and lived a rough life. His dad left when he was just a baby, and his mom had to work two jobs just to feed the two of them. He was on his own most of the time. He had to be tough to make it in his neighborhood, and as he got older, he became very angry.

When he was 12, he joined his neighborhood gang. He threw himself into the gang life—stealing, fighting, and killing. By the time he was 15, he had seen it all. One day, he met a man at a youth mission who really cared about him—Jorge. Jorge had lived the life so he knew what Carlos was going through. By spending time with Jorge, Carlos realized that he was tired of all of the violence, of watching his back, of hurting his mom. He wanted what Jorge had.

Carlos became a Christian. When he did this, he knew that he had to give up the gang life, because it was not what he was about anymore. He also knew what would happen to him if he left. His homeboys were already suspicious because he hadn't been hanging out with them as much. He also had seen what happened to his friends who tried to leave. The gang had beaten most of them so badly that many did not live. Still, Carlos knew that he wanted to get out of the gang, no matter what he had to go through.

When it came time for his beating, Jorge was there. Not only was he there, but as the gang members were lifting their clubs, Jorge stood in front of Carlos. He begged them to just let Carlos go. They refused. So Jorge did the unbelievable. He said, "Let me take his place."

"What?" they laughed. "Are you stupid, man?"

"No. Let me take his place."

They did. Jorge received Carlos's beating. He stood in Carlos's place. Like many others who had been beaten, Jorge did not walk away that day. Carlos was never the same because he realized that Jorge loved him enough to die in his place.

Bridge: "Jorge took Carlos's place. What an awesome thing to do for someone! In Old Testament times, God required a sacrifice to take the place of the people's sins. They offered animals on an altar as a way to pay for their sins—to atone for them."

Book Use the stone altar to briefly explain the reason for animal sacrifices. Explain that God required it to pay for the sins of the people, and explain that the animal had to be perfect, without any blemish.

Read Hebrews 9:27–28. Explain that Jesus took the place of animal sacrifices. He became the lamb who was slain for the atonement of our sins. Use the *cross* (in your pocket) as a visual aid. Next, play the "Secret Ambition" music video.

Bridge: "Remember the story about Jorge and Carlos? Remember how you felt when you heard that Jorge took his place? Jesus did that for us. He died the worst possible death so that we might have eternal life."

Look Have a student give a testimony about how he or she came to know Jesus. This student should also tell the difference that being born again has made in his or her life.

Bridge: "Some of you here know this and believe this. What I want to ask you is whether you are living with an 'attitude of gratitude' for your salvation. Or do you just take it for granted? Do you need to recommit to living for your Savior tonight?

"Others of you here have never accepted Jesus as Savior. He loves you. He died for you! Jesus took your place! Do you want to choose to live for him tonight?

"Still others of you have questions. You may not be sure if this Christianity stuff is for you. We want you to know that having questions is okay. We love you. God loves you. We are here for you if you want to talk to us or ask us questions."

Took During this time, leaders will be responsible for talking with each student who will receive one of the following items: committed Christians will receive a power bracelet; recommitted Christians will receive a power bracelet; new believers will receive a cross necklace and a New Believer packet; seekers will receive a "cross in my pocket."

Ask students to sit quietly. The worship band will play softly until all of the students have talked with a leader.

Afterwards, leaders should meet together to discuss any important information that students shared. Pray for the students. Celebrate the new believers!

Lesson Plan 9

"Let's (Really!) Talk"

by Gloria Chang

Objective

By the end of an hour lesson on Genesis 24:67 and 27:1–17, students will analyze effective communication in marriage by identifying reasons for poor communication between Isaac and Rebekah and by memorizing Proverbs 15:4. [Analysis]

For Chinese Married Couples

Nook As students enter, play one or two popular love songs familiar to this age group. Ask married couples to pray with their spouses that their relationship will be strengthened today as a result of the lesson they are about to learn.

Hook Play an episode of *I Love Lucy* that features Lucy planning an elaborate scheme to deceive her husband, Ricky. After viewing, point out features of bad communication to your class. Ask students for positive and negative aspects of this couple's communication. List them on the board in two columns. As you do so, note the emotions— fear, frustration, and anger—underlying the communication. Be prepared to share an example from your own marriage.

Bridge: "Most of Ricky and Lucy's communication is bad communication. But we can learn a lot about good communication if we study poor communication. Many of us are guilty of making many of the same mistakes, but it's more difficult to laugh at ourselves. Once we become aware of our mistakes, we can look for ways to improve so that we will not make the same errors again. In the book of Genesis, we find a very old example of bad communication in a marriage."

Book Read Genesis 24:67 and 27:1–17. Then divide the class into three groups. The first group will answer the question, "What kind of relationship did Isaac and Rebekah have when they were first married?" (Gen. 24:67). The second group will answer the question, "What kind of communication did Isaac use later in life?" (chap. 27).

Materials Checklist
- Bibles
- Clips of *I Love Lucy* (taped from television)
- TV/VCR
- White board and markers
- Overhead projector
- Three blank transparencies
- Paper and pens for students

The third group will answer the question, "In the end, how did Rebekah communicate with Isaac?"

The groups will report their observations to the full class using the overhead projector. Conclude by noting how Isaac and Rebekah initially had a very good relationship that gradually fell apart in their middle years so much so that when they were old, their communication style was completely unhealthy.

Bridge: "What went wrong?"

Look Display transparencies that list ways of responding to conflict and under a separate column, the feelings behind poor communication. Among them are:

Denial	Fatigue
Repression	Irritability
Suppression	Tension
Postponement	Fear
Abusive Language	Anger
Physical Violence	Weakness
Intellectualism	Concealing Emotions

Ask the class to return to their groups and evaluate Isaac and Rebecca after considering these two lists.

Took Divide the class again, this time into dyads—one couple—a husband-and-wife team. Ask each person to individually list his or her spouse's likes and dislikes (limit three each!). Also, list one main communication difficulty. Ask the couple to compare their lists. Do they agree? Why? Why not?

For the coming week, challenge the students with the following assignment: If they find themselves engaged in poor communication, note what occurred, and at an appropriate time, discuss what they could have done differently with their spouse.

Memorize: Proverbs 15:4—"The tongue that brings healing is a tree of life, but a deceitful tongue crushes the spirit."

Cook Next week we will continue our study on developing a strong marriage by looking at how we communicate with our children. Pay attention this week, and return to class with your observations and questions.

Appendix B
Sample Forms

Answer Key to Show, Tell, Do

	SHOW Visual	TELL Auditory	DO Kinesthetic
1. Conduct a demonstration			X
2. Display a clip from television	X		
3. Do no-talk teacher			X
4. Prepare a speech or lecture		X	
5. Use an overhead projector	X		
6. Have small-group discussion		X	
7. Complete this story		X	
8. Write a skit or play	X		
9. Play games			X
10. Take a trip			X
11. Make a poster	X		
12. Listen to a testimony		X	
13. Sing a solo or group song		X	
14. Go for a hospital visit			X
15. Listen to a song on a CD		X	
16. Draw or color	X		
17. Visualize or imagine	X		
18. Paraphrase a passage	X		
19. Read in unison		X	
20. Do question-and-answer		X	
21. Discuss in neighbor nudge		X	
22. Cook a meal/eat a meal			X
23. Say a sentence prayer		X	
24. Conduct an interview		X	
25. Have a puppet show		X	
26. Keep a journal	X		
27. Tell an account with flannelgraph	X		
28. See a movie	X		
29. Complete a puzzle			X
30. Play the Bible drill			X
31. Memorize a verse		X	
32. Repeat the Bible account		X	
33. Make arts and crafts			X
34. Take a test	X		
35. Find the Scripture	X		
36. Write a letter	X		

	SHOW Visual	TELL Auditory	DO Kinesthetic
37. Agree/disagree discussion		X	
38. Unscramble the verses	X		
39. Listen to a tape recording		X	
40. Take a walk			X
41. Find locations on a map	X		
42. Unscramble the words	X		
43. Play instruments		X	
44. Answer in circle response		X	
45. Post on bulletin board	X		
46. Finger paint			X
47. Do a dramatic reading		X	
48. Compose a poem	X		
49. Give a ten-minute sermon		X	
50. Dress up as a Bible character			X
51. Paraphrase a hymn		X	
52. Write a commercial	X		
53. Do spontaneous drama			X
54. Make a collage	X		
55. Brainstorm		X	
56. Write poetry/psalm	X		
57. Write out a Bible verse	X		
58. Dialogue		X	
59. Make a mural	X		
60. Do role-play			X
61. Debate		X	
62. Make charts			X
63. Write a prayer	X		
64. Compare songs		X	
65. Pantomime			X
66. Record a report	X		
67. Write a character comparison	X		
68. Solve a problem		X	
69. Do creative writing	X		
70. Make a video	X		
71. Perform a sociodrama (social problem)			X
72. Write original songs		X	
73. Paint			X
74. Do paper cuts			X
75. Make a mobile			X

Volunteer Application

[Attach your photo here]

Date: _____

Name _____ Telephone # ( ) _____ ( ) _____
Address _____ City _____ Zip Code _____
Age _____ Birthday _____ Marital Status _____
Are you CPR certified, or do you have any medical training? _____
Describe your experience with children (paid or volunteer): _____
_____
_____

How long have you attended our church? (If less than one year, list previous church name, address, and phone number.) _____
Have you completed New Members/When? _____ 7 Laws?_____
Have you taken the Spiritual Gifts Class? _____
In what church ministries do you participate on a regular basis?_____
_____

Please check your preference: ❑ Nursery   ❑ Preschool   ❑ Grades 1–5   ❑ Jr. Light Co. (6–8 grade)   ❑ Youth Church   ❑ Children's Bible Study   ❑ Childcare   ❑ Tutoring
Statement of faith (when were you saved?) _____
_____
_____

References (List 3 people who have known you 5 years or longer.)
1. Name _____ Telephone _____(Day)
   Address _____ City _____ Zip Code _____
2. Name _____ Telephone _____(Day)
   Address _____ City _____ Zip Code _____
3. Name _____ Telephone _____(Day)
   Address _____ City _____ Zip Code _____

Have you ever been convicted of a crime? _____ Have you ever been fingerprinted? _____
To maintain the safety of our children, every applicant must be fingerprinted at the Inglewood Police Department. The fee of $15.00 is to be paid by you personally. Attach proof of fingerprint.

Applicant's Signature _____ **Date** _____
Pastoral Approval _____ **Date** _____

Letter of Commitment

By signing this document, I hereby commit to serving in Children's Church for one year as _____ .

I am volunteering in the following area(s): _____
_____
_____ .

As part of my responsibility to this ministry, I will regularly attend monthly Teachers' Meetings and avail myself of training whenever possible. I further commit to daily personal prayer and Bible study time to grow closer in my fellowship with the Lord.

As a leader, I will serve as a godly example and role model to the children. As a child of God, I will maintain a lifestyle in keeping with biblical standards. I pledge to serve with excellence as a member of the Christian education team, always mindful that I am responsible for teaching God's special gifts—the children.

Name _____

Signature _____

Date _____

NURSERY SIGN-IN

PLEASE PRINT

DATE: _____

Child's Name	Age	Parent's Name	Pick-up Signature

PRESCHOOL SIGN-IN

PLEASE PRINT

DATE: _____

Child's Name	Age	Parent's Name	Pick-up Signature

KINDERGARTEN SIGN-IN

PLEASE PRINT

DATE: _____

Child's Name	Age	Parent's Name	Pick-up Signature

CHILDREN'S CHURCH SIGN-IN

PLEASE PRINT

DATE: _____

Child's Name									

Parent's Signature									

Baby Dedication Decision Form

Your Name and Address

_____

_____

Telephone ( ) _____

YOUR COMMITMENT: Please check all statements that apply to you.

To be the parents and godparents God has called us to be, we must live clean lives and try every day to be more like him. To do this we must accept him as our personal Savior and have a close relationship with him.

❏ I AM NOW ACCEPTING CHRIST AS MY PERSONAL SAVIOR FOR THE FIRST TIME.

❏ I HAVE QUESTIONS AND WOULD LIKE TO SPEAK TO SOMEONE.

❏ I AM RECOMMITTING MY LIFE TO JESUS CHRIST.

❏ I AM INTERESTED IN BECOMING A MEMBER OF THIS CHURCH.

❏ I AM INTERESTED IN COMPLETING NEW MEMBERS CLASS.

❏ I AM INTERESTED IN ATTENDING A BIBLE STUDY.

❏ I WILL ATTEND SUNDAY MORNING SERVICE REGULARLY.

❏ I PROMISE TO KEEP MY TEMPLE PURE ACCORDING TO ROMANS 12:1–2 AND PRAY THAT GOD WILL HELP ME TO NOT HAVE SEX OUTSIDE OF MARRIAGE.

❏ I WILL READ MY BIBLE AND PRAY DAILY.

Your Relationship to Baby

_____

Baby Dedication Form

I prayed for this child,
And the LORD has granted me what I asked of him.
So now I give him to the LORD.
For his whole life he will be given over to the LORD.
1 Samuel 1:27–28

Congratulations on your decision to dedicate your child to the LORD! The Baby Dedication Service is held the *fifth* Sunday of the month during the 5:00 p.m. service. Please complete the form below with the information that you would like to appear on the Baby Dedication Certificate. *Please print legibly.*

Baby's Name _____

Date of Birth _____ City _____ State _____

Mother's Name _____

Father's Name _____

Godmother's Name _____

Godfather's Name _____

Check the color certificate you desire: ❏ pink   ❏ blue   ❏ red   ❏ green

Mailing Address: _____

_____

Telephone: _____ (Day)

_____ (Evening)

PRAYER FOR BABY DEDICATION

As the families stand in front, the pastor leads the church in this prayer.

Children ages 12 and below are asked to stand and repeat:

> "I pray for these babies,
> that as they grow in their childhood,
> they would know the love of Christ,
> they would show the love of Christ,
> and they would grow in the love of Christ.
> I pray for them in the name of
> the Father, Son, and Holy Spirit."

Children are seated, and teenagers are asked to stand and repeat:

> "I pray for these babies,
> that as they grow in their youth,
> they would know the love of Christ,
> they would show the love of Christ,
> and they would grow in the love of Christ.
> I pray for them in the name of
> the Father, Son, and Holy Spirit."

Teenagers are seated, and adults are asked to stand and repeat:

> "I pray for these babies,
> that as they grow in their adulthood,
> they would know the love of Christ,
> they would show the love of Christ,
> and they would grow in the love of Christ.
> I pray for them in the name of
> the Father, Son, and Holy Spirit."

Adults remain standing, and everyone is asked to stand and repeat:

> "With God's help, I will walk uprightly before them.
> With God's help, I will live a godly example before them.
> I pray for these babies in the name of
> the Father, Son, and Holy Spirit.
> Amen."

As prayed by Bishop Kenneth C. Ulmer, Pastor-Teacher, Faithful Central Missionary Baptist Church

Your Child's First Communion

Dear Parents,

    Communion is a special ordinance that our Lord Jesus Christ instituted. We identify with Christ through baptism, and we take Communion "in remembrance of him."

    Your child has accepted Jesus Christ as Savior and has expressed a desire to participate in this ordinance. On Sunday, _____, we will have a special Communion class at 11:00. Please come with your child to _____ (room) in the _____ (building).

    During this class, children will learn the meaning of Communion in terms they can understand. We will teach parents how to reinforce at home what has been taught about Communion. Therefore, we ask that parents attend this one-hour class with their child.

    The First Communion service will be on Sunday, _____, during the 5 p.m. service in the main sanctuary. All children will also be presented with a gift at that time to commemorate this special event. Please complete the form below and return it to the church office. If you have any questions, please do not hesitate to call the Ministry of Christian Education at _____ (phone number).

- -

First Communion Registration

Child's Name _____

Parents' Names _____

Children's Church Teacher _____

Child's Age _____ Grade in School _____

Mailing Address _____

        City _____ State _____ Zip Code _____

Phone Number _____ (Daytime)

               _____ (Evening)

[Adapted from the Crystal Cathedral Children's Ministry, 1320 Chapman Avenue, Garden Grove, CA 92640]

Certificate of Communion

Is not the cup of thanksgiving for which we give thanks
a participation ion the blood of Christ?
And is not the bread that we break
a participation in the body of Christ?
Because there is one loaf, we, who are many,
are one body, for we all partake of the one loaf.
1 Corinthians 10:16–17

This certifies that

_____

Name

joined the congregation at the Lord's Table
on this_____day of_____ in the year _____

_____

Senior Pastor

_____

Pastor of Christian Education

_____

Congregation

_____

Address

_____

City/State

TRAVEL PERMISSION FORM

ALL BLANK SPACES MUST BE FILLED IN!

    I hereby grant (church name) _____ permission to transport my son/daughter to and from the church to (the destination) _____ _____ for (name of the event) _____.

    I have instructed my child to obey the teachers, leaders, and adult volunteers. There are no drugs or weapons in my child's possession. All music and headphones have been left at home.

    My son/daughter has the following medical need or illness _____ (write none if none) and has _____ medication (write none if none). Our medical insurance carrier is _____, and my child has the medical insurance card. The number is _____.

    In the event of an emergency, you may call or page me at ( )_____. In the event of an accident, I will not hold (church name) _____ liable.

    The bus is due to arrive back at the church by (time of arrival) _____. I will be there promptly to pick up my child.

Parent's signature: _____

Name and age of child/children: _____ Age _____
_____ Age _____
_____ Age _____

Authorization and Consent to Treat Minor

The above-signed do hereby authorize the directors/teachers of _____ _____, as agents for the above-signed, to consent to any X-ray examination, anesthetic, medical, dental, or surgical diagnosis or treatment and hospital care for the above minor that is deemed advisable by and to be rendered under the general or special supervision of any physician and surgeon licensed under the provision of the Medicine Practice Act or any dentist licensed under the Dental Practice Act, at a hospital or elsewhere. The above-mentioned agent is authorized to make decisions concerning the health and general welfare of this minor. This authorization will remain effective while the above minor is in the care of the above agents for an indefinite period unless otherwise revoked in writing by the above-signed and delivered to the directors/teachers of _____. First aid and nonprescription medications will be administered to the above-mentioned minor at the direction of the directors/teachers or their health care representatives with the following exceptions:

❑ No Exceptions
❑ Exceptions _____

Medication that the above-mentioned minor is required to take will be turned over to the camp nurse or health care representatives. Type of medication and specific instructions:

_____

_____

Activity restrictions and/or allergies, including reactions to medication, are as follows:

_____

_____

| _____ | _____ |
| Parent or Guardian Signature | Witness |

```
┌─────────────────────────────────────────────────┐
│  ┌───────────────────────────────────────────┐  │
│  │           Church Letterhead               │  │
│  │      Address • Telephone Number           │  │
│  │          Name of Pastor(s)                │  │
│  └───────────────────────────────────────────┘  │
└─────────────────────────────────────────────────┘
```

Baptism Form

Repent, and be baptized every one of you,
In the name of Jesus Christ
For the remission of sins,
And ye shall receive the gift of the Holy Ghost.
Acts 2:38 KJV

Congratulations on your decision to be baptized!

On the day of baptism, a deacon or deaconess will take you to dress for baptism. Please bring with you a change of underclothes (you must be fully dressed because the baptism gowns are sheer when wet), a white, long tee-shirt or tee-shirt and shorts, a bathing cap if needed, and a towel.

Please complete the following information, *printed legibly,* with the information that you would like to appear on the Baptism Certificate. Following baptism, you will dress and return to the service. You will receive your certificate, which is a legal document, at the close of the service.

Your Full Name (include your middle name) _____

Date of Birth _____ Place of Birth _____

We also need the following information:

Mailing Address:

Mr. / Mrs. / Ms. _____

Street Address _____

City/State _____ Zip Code _____

Day Phone (   ) _____ Evening (   ) _____

Age _____ Date Joined _____

Have you completed New Members classes? ❑ Yes   ❑ No

Everything You Need to Know About Baptism

But when they believed Philip,
Preaching the things concerning
The kingdom of God, and the name of Jesus Christ,
They were baptized, both men and women.
Acts 8:12 KJV

Faithful Central Missionary Baptist Church
333 West Florence Avenue
Inglewood, California 90301
(310) 330–8000

Bishop Kenneth C. Ulmer, Ph.D., D.Min.
Pastor-Teacher

La Verne A. Tolbert, Ph.D.
Pastor of Christian Education

COMMONLY ASKED QUESTIONS

1. **What does the word "baptism" mean?**

   Baptism comes from a Greek word, *baptizo*, which means "to dip or to immerse." In Matthew 28:19, baptism is commanded by Jesus Christ.

   Therefore go and make disciples of all nations,
   baptizing them in the name of the Father and of the Son
   and of the Holy Spirit. (NIV)

2. **What if I was baptized as a baby?**

   If you were baptized before you accepted Jesus Christ as your Lord and Savior, you were just a baby who got a little wet. Since a baby cannot confess faith in God, babies are not baptized according to the examples that we see in the Bible. Jesus was baptized as an adult, not as a baby (Luke 3:21–23). Another example is the account of the Ethiopian eunuch (Acts 8:26–38). The Bible gives the divine order that belief precedes baptism.

3. **What does baptism symbolize?**

Baptism symbolizes that you identify with the death, burial, and resurrection of Jesus Christ. It is your public confession. Baptism tells the world that you now have a new life. Your old life is over, gone, dead. Baptism is an outward act portraying an inward change (Romans 6:1–23; 2 Corinthians 5:17).

4. **What if I sin after I'm baptized? Do I need to be baptized again?**

Jesus Christ forgives sin once and for all. If we do sin, we confess our sin. A Christian does not have a lifestyle of habitual, continual, deliberate sin (1 John 1:7–10; 3:9).

5. **What significance is there between baptism and the church?**

Symbolically, baptism identifies us with Christ and with the church. As we are united with Christ, the Head of the church, we are united to his body, the church, called also the body of Christ (Ephesians 1:22–23; 1 Corinthians 12:12–14, 24–27).

6. **What responsibility do I have to the church?**

Since we are one body, we are to fellowship with one another. This means that regular church attendance is a must. To become an active member of this church body, attend New Members class. Those who really want to grow and learn will also attend a Bible study (Hebrews 10:24–25).

7. **Don't neglect your daily time with the Lord.**

Reading your Bible and praying daily will help you to know and to understand God's Word. Your relationship with God through Jesus Christ is personal; communication—prayer—is key (Proverbs 8:17)!

WHAT IS COMMUNION?

Communion is a special ordinance (or custom) of the church. Only those who are believers participate in what is commonly called the Lord's Supper (1 Corinthians 11:23–34).

Communion is a time for us to remember that our salvation was purchased with the death and resurrection of Jesus Christ. The bread (or cracker) symbolizes his body that was beaten and bruised for our sins. The wine (or juice) symbolizes the blood that flowed when they placed the thorny crown into his skull, when the nails were hammered into his hands and feet, and when the spear pierced his side.

Here is power for victorious living! It is in Jesus, not in ourselves. All we need to do is give our lives to him and ask him to live his life through us. When we take Communion, it is a time for us to reflect upon our lives. To realize the extent of God's love for us, and to renew our commitment to holy living through the power of the Cross.

You were bought with a price;
Therefore glorify God in your body.
1 Corinthians 6:20 NRSV

Bibliography

Colson, Howard P., and M. Raymond. *Understanding Your Church's Curriculum*. Nashville: Broadman Press, 1981.

Creative Bible Learning for Young Children. Ventura, CA: Regal Books, 1977.

Gangel, Kenneth O. *Twenty-four Ways to Improve Your Teaching*. Wheaton, IL: Victor Books, 1988.

Gangel, Kenneth O., and Howard G. Hendricks. *The Christian Educator's Handbook on Teaching*. Wheaton, IL: Victor Books, 1989.

Guild, Pat Burke, and Stephen Garger. *Marching to Different Drummers*. Alexandria, VA: Association for Supervision and Curriculum Development, 1985.

LeBar, Lois. *Education That Is Christian*. Wheaton, IL: Victor Books, 1989.

Mager, Robert F. *Preparing Instructional Objectives*. Belmont, CA: Fearon Publishers, 1961.

Richards, Lawrence O. *Creative Bible Teaching*. Chicago: Moody Press, 1970.

_____. *A Theology of Christian Education*. Grand Rapids: Zondervan, 1975.

Roe, Earl, O., editor. *Dream Big: The Henrietta Mears Story*. Ventura, CA: Regal Books, 1990.

Tyler, Ralph W. *Basic Principles of Curriculum and Instruction*. Chicago: University of Chicago Press, 1949.

Welter, Paul. *How to Help a Friend*. Wheaton, IL: Tyndale, 1975.

Subject and Name Index